CW01391072

Mindful
Travel

INSPIRING SPIRITUAL DESTINATIONS
FROM AROUND THE WORLD

ALICE PECK

CICO BOOKS

For Duane and Tyl, still …

This edition published in 2025 by CICO Books
An imprint of Ryland Peters & Small Ltd

20–21 Jockey's Fields   1452 Davis Bugg Road
London WC1R 4BW   Warrenton, NC 27589

www.rylandpeters.com
Email: euregulations@rylandpeters.com

10 9 8 7 6 5 4 3 2 1

First published in 2022 as *Around the World in 80 Spiritual Places.*

Text © Alice Peck 2022, 2025

Design and illustration © CICO Books 2022, 2025

For photography credits, see page 159.

The author's moral rights have been asserted.
All rights reserved. No part of this publication
may be reproduced, stored in a retrieval system,
or transmitted in any form or by any means,
electronic, mechanical, photocopying, or otherwise,
without the prior permission of the publisher.

A CIP record for this book is available from the
British Library.
US Library of Congress CIP data has been applied for.

ISBN: 978-1-80065-432-7

Printed in China

Editor: Rosie Fairhead
Commissioning editor: Kristine Pidkameny
Senior commissioning editor: Carmel Edmonds
Senior designer: Emily Breen
Art director: Sally Powell
Creative director: Leslie Harrington
Production manager: Gordana Simakovic
Publishing manager: Penny Craig
Publisher: Cindy Richards

The authorised representative in the EEA is
Authorised Rep Compliance Ltd.,
Ground Floor. 71 Lower Baggot Street,
Dublin, D01 P593, Ireland
www.arccompliance.com

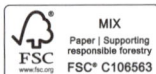

FSC
www.fsc.org

MIX
Paper | Supporting
responsible forestry
FSC® C106563

Contents

Introduction

Places are not inherently spiritual. We imbue them with mysticism and mystery. The sacred reveals itself when we pause, become mindfully present, and experience a sense of unity—a shift that brings wonder, acceptance, awe, or healing. My sacred places include Schoolhouse Pond in Chatham, Massachusetts, where my son delighted in his first swim; Lafayette Park in downtown Detroit, where I shared adolescent dreams with my best friend; Green-Wood Cemetery, where my husband and I have spent countless seasons rambling; and the paths and piers by the harbor in Red Hook, Brooklyn, where we walk every morning. There, the geese and herons join us, humid breezes carry after-storm calm, berries ripen, and bee-filled hibiscus hum, as the tides deliver both grim fish-kills and bright ducklings.

To travel mindfully means to be fully present to a place, receiving it as it is without imposing our ideas or expectations. In doing so, we connect with something far greater than ourselves—something we might call sacred. Whether we visit a new country, explore a neighborhood, or take a different route to a familiar spot, we know that stepping into a place for the first time, returning to it over and over, or simply observing its layers of past and present can change us. That change, I believe, is inherently spiritual.

This is the heart of my definition of spiritual places. While researching this book, I encountered many perspectives on how to travel mindfully, but my favorite comes from T.C. McLuhan, who wrote in *Cathedrals of the Spirit* about "Landscapes of the holy … centers of inspiration where human consciousness is temporarily set free." When our consciousness is freed—when we release our biases,

expectations, and our feelings and memories—we can simply be
with a place. That is mindful traveling. It is in this state of presence
that allows the sacred, mystical, or profound to be revealed.

As I chose from the infinite spiritual places in the cosmos,
I considered the spans of time, geography, and the people who
have found sustenance, peace, inspiration, or even magic in these

locations. I believe in liminal or thin places—those spaces between heaven and earth, dream and reality, sacred and mundane. This idea is echoed through these pages, shaped by insights of inspiring writers—Charles Foster, Marilynne Robinson, Matsuo Bashō, Diana Eck, Jalāl al-Dīn Rūmī, Nikos Kazantzakis, Max Roach, Huston Smith—and sacred texts from the Buddha to the Bible, the Qur'an to the Bhagavad Gita. I also drew wisdom from friends, editors, and meditation teachers.

I've aimed to take the ideas of the sacred and spiritual out of denominational boundaries, making them universal—or at least universally relatable—often grounding them in the web of nature.

At the same time, I've sought to honor the line between celebration and inspiration versus appropriation. This book is not a guidebook but rather a dream book—subjective and selective, yet aspirational. Meditations, prayers, and contemplations are woven in to foster mindfulness and offer meaningful experiences, even if physical travel is out of reach.

Wherever we go—Mount Kailash or the local greengrocer, a cathedral or a graveyard—and however we get there, whether by pilgrim's walk or city bus, we can travel mindfully. Ultimately, the destination, as poet Jacques Prévert so beautifully puts it, is the "sweet present of the present."

CHAPTER 1

EUROPE

GIANT'S CAUSEWAY
County Antrim, Northern Ireland, UK

Stonehenge

The Saxons called it Stonehenge or the Hanging Stones; medieval writers sang of the Giant's Dance. Was it built as a Roman or Druid temple? A zodiacal temple? A site for pilgrimage? Phoenicians, Mycenaeans, Romans, Saxons, Danes, and even the mythical enchanter Merlin have been linked to this place. Sometimes spirituality is found in mystery, and perhaps that is what draws more than 800,000 yearly visitors.

A specter of what it must have first been when newly constructed, Stonehenge is still the most epic of Britain's 1,300 stone circles. The site is the only Neolithic monument in the British Isles to consist of boulders that were not sourced locally, and many of them weigh as much as 25 tons. The main ring of sandstone monoliths stands 13 ft (4 m) high, linked by lintels surrounding a circle of 16-ft-tall (5 m) bluestones from Wales, as well as other structures encompassing the altar stone and burial mounds. Regardless of its spiritual purpose, Stonehenge is a miracle of transportation, engineering, and construction.

Some researchers have demonstrated how the stones align with the planets and solstices, and may therefore have constituted a prehistoric observatory, but others disagree. Perhaps one day we will know the answer, but until then we may still appreciate the mystery of the place.

Marvel at the night sky

Consider the astrophysicist Neil deGrasse Tyson's reflection in *Death by Black Hole, and Other Cosmic Quandaries* (2007): "We are too busy watching evening television to care what is going on in the sky. To us, a simple rock alignment based on cosmic patterns looks like an Einsteinian feat. But a truly mysterious civilization would be one that made no cultural or architectural reference to the sky at all." Observe the night sky and take Tyson's words to heart as you notice the marvels of the galaxy.

Glastonbury

There are as many legends about the town of Glastonbury and the surrounding area as there are attendees at its world-famous music festival—about 200,000 visitors for five days in June—but what is certain is that it is the site of some of England's earliest Christian structures built by the Saxons and rebuilt many times since. Parts of a church, two chapels, and a freestanding abbot's kitchen remain.

Some believe that Glastonbury is the true location of King Arthur's legendary Avalon, that he was buried there with his queen Guinevere, and that the Holy Grail—lost since the Last Supper—is hidden deep within the Chalice Well. At the base of Glastonbury Tor (a rocky crag that is also called Blood Spring because the surge of the water is said to sound like a heart beating and the water is tinged red with iron oxide), this well is thought to be the site of Merlin's Cave, hiding an entrance to a fairy palace.

Nearby, a hawthorn tree known as the Glastonbury thorn blooms at Christmas. It is said that it or its ancestor took root when Joseph of Arimathea drove his staff—perhaps carved from the wood of Jesus' Cross—into the ground near the well. Legend says that he visited Glastonbury with Jesus Christ when he was a young man, and after the Crucifixion buried holy relics here.

Be still and listen

Despite the intrigues, disputes, and burdens of history and the number of tourists who crowd a famous destination, sometimes it is best to be still, listen, and let the place speak to us. Listen for the heartbeat of the place. Perhaps that's the lesson of Glastonbury.

Giant's Causeway

These dramatic cliffs above the Atlantic Ocean are a thing of wonder, and have sparked the imagination of poets, geologists, naturalists, and artists for centuries. According to legend, the basalt columns that look like huge stepping stones from land to sea were built by a giant or folk hero named Fionn Mac Cumhaill (Finn McCool). Geologists, however, are in agreement that these 40,000 interlocking columns were created by a volcanic eruption during the Paleocene Epoch (66–56 million years ago). Molten basalt passed through chalk beds, and as the lava cooled it contracted, creating the myriad columns. Although most of these are hexagonal, some have as many as eight sides, and the tallest are 39 ft (12 m) high.

The Blue Trail is the most popular, but if you walk along the less-trafficked clifftops toward Runkerry Beach, on the line of the Bushmills Heritage Railway, you will have an amazing view not only of the causeway, but also of Scotland and the Republic of Ireland's Inishowen Peninsula. Along this section of the railway you might spot some rare sea spleenwort and frog orchids. As if the remarkable geological formations were not enough, the Giant's Causeway is also a nature reserve where plants and birds—breeding skylarks, stonechats, and linnets among them—are protected.

Amazing world, indeed

Spend some time with the lines the poet William Hamilton Drummond wrote in 1811:

> What roots of rock thick woven, and entwined,
> Those giant steps to earth's fixed centre bind;
> What seaborn forests clothe their vallied sides,
> What Whirling pools absorb th' engulfing tides;
> How Maelstrom rages on Norwegian shores,
> Or Corry Vreckan's frightful vortex roars.
> Amazing world!

Isle of Skye

At 639 sq. miles (1,656 sq. km), the Isle of Skye is the northernmost and one of the largest islands of the Inner Hebrides. It has been inhabited by Picts, Celts, and Norse peoples. In their sagas, the Norse referred to the island as Skýey or Skuyö—"Isle of Clouds"—and a poetic Gaelic name for the island is Eilean a' Cheò, meaning "Island of the Mist."

Skye's architecture reflects its many inhabitants, and the brochs—Pictish round towers built more than 2,000 years ago—are especially compelling. Dunvegan Castle is the oldest inhabited castle in Scotland, and there are churches and other historical structures, but what makes it a spiritual destination for me is the island itself—its craggy, atmospheric mountains, labyrinthine shoreline, fossils, unique wildlife (including the rare white-tailed sea eagle), misty vistas, and flora. Especially compelling are the Fairy Pools clustered at the base of the Black Cuillin mountains near the village of Carbost, where clear, icy water flows down into the glen, spilling into rockpools of aquamarine blue.

It has been said that inhabitants of the Isle of Skye possess "second sight," as explained by the sixteenth-century writer Donald Monro in his *Description of the Western Isles of Scotland*:

Connect to a thin place

The beauty of the mists, mountains, and glassy pools is so compelling that it is no surprise Skye is believed to be another "thin place," in which the distance between human and holy closes. Take a moment, no matter where you are, to settle quietly and breathe consciously. See if you can connect to a thin place. It might be external—perhaps a connection to nature, or internal—such as a feeling of love or ease.

"The Second Sight is a singular faculty of seeing an otherwise invisible object, without any previous means used by the person that sees it for that end; the vision makes such a lively impression upon the seers, that they neither see nor think of anything else, except the vision, as long as it continues; and then they appear pensive or jovial, according to the object which was represented to them." It is believed that those with the gift lose it when they travel to the mainland. Perhaps that is true, but what is certain is that after experiencing Skye's beauty, it is hard to shake off the impression.

Clarity on Skye is not just for water and mind. The night firmament, especially when seen from the northwestern coast near Glendale, is so devoid of human-made light that the stars are startlingly visible. In fact, so many are visible that it can be a challenge to distinguish familiar constellations.

Newgrange

Newgrange or Sí an Bhrú is on the north side of the River Boyne, to the north of Dublin. It was constructed from approximately 200,000 tons of rock, and the main structure is Neolithic, dating from about 3200 BCE. It is older than Stonehenge (see page 10) or the pyramids in Egypt, although additions were made during the Iron Age and early Christian era. The stone building covered with grass looks like a verdant spaceship, but it is a mound containing a stone-lined passage leading to several inner chambers. Within, archaeologists have discovered human remains and what may be grave offerings.

Encircling the mound are pockets of white quartz and 97 huge stones covered in megalithic symbols and inscriptions. Some of them were transported from as far away as the Wicklow Mountains, about 60 miles (100 km) to the south. The American writer Burton E. Stevenson described these carvings in *The Charm of Ireland* in 1914: "It was noticeable that there was no attempt at any general

Light after dark

Each year, on December 21, visitors gather here to await dawn on the winter solstice, as reverent and curious folk have done for millennia. Imagine the awe and wonder ancient peoples must have experienced, waiting in the darkness for the longest night of the year to give way to light.

scheme of decoration, for the spirals and coils were scattered here and there without any reference to each other, some of them in inaccessible corners which proved they had been made before the stones were placed in position. Evidently, they had been carved wherever the whim of the sculptor suggested; and so, in spite of their delicacy and beauty, they are in a way supremely childish."

But there is nothing childish about the tomb itself. Nobody knows from what forgotten quarry these great slabs—many of them weighing more than 100 tons—were cut. Wherever it was, they had to be dragged to the top of this hill before being set in position.

Historians disagree about the purpose of the structure, but it was likely some sort of temple or other place of worship. Every year,

with extraordinary accuracy, an opening in the roof aligns with the sunrise of the winter solstice. As the sun moves upward, the beam expands until the entire inner chamber is illuminated, perhaps with the intention of symbolizing the triumph of good over evil, or life over death.

Newgrange and the neighboring Knowth and Dowth comprise Brú na Bóinne (Mansion of the Boyne). The monuments of this site, according to UNESCO, represent the largest and most important expression of prehistoric megalithic art in Europe.

La Forêt de Soignes

Also known as the Sonian Forest and the Beech Cathedral, this 10,920-acre (4,420-ha.) woodland on the southeastern edge of Brussels is comprised mainly of European beeches and oak, many of them more than 200 years old.

The French sculptor Auguste Rodin made frequent trips to the area while living in Brussels during the 1870s, and completed several paintings of the forest. Perhaps he was thinking of La Forêt de Soignes when, in conversation with the art critic Paul Gsell, he commented: "It is not only in living beings that [the landscape painter] sees the reflection of the universal soul; it is in the trees, the bushes, the valleys, the hills … Everywhere the great artist hears spirit answer to his spirit."

Such qualities have struck not just poets and artists. Monks and nuns throughout the centuries have sought spiritual refuge in convents and cloisters in and near forests, but what makes this one special are the standing stones, dolmen, which look as though they belong at Stonehenge or perhaps Newgrange (see pages 10 and 19).

In the heart of the forest, a huge stone surrounded by 11 more stands at the end of a path. If you look closely, you will see inscriptions: not megalithic symbols, but the names of Belgian forestry workers who lost their lives in World War One. Erected in the 1920s, it is a way to unite people from all over Belgium who died for their country, in a landscape they surely loved.

The beauty of nature

How does being in nature make you feel? More than 20 types of lichen, many mosses, and over 1,000 species of mushroom grow in the Sonian Forest. The mushrooms are natural composters, important for breaking down organic material (such as leaves) and sustaining both animals and trees. They are a reminder of Rodin's famous words, "To the artist, all in nature is beautiful." This could be said for the spiritual seeker as well. As I often put it, "Nature is my church."

Hala Sultan Tekke

Sufism is (at least outwardly) the most mystical form of Islam. About a century after the Prophet Muhammad's death, Sufis split away from their fellow Muslims, shunning worldliness and pursuing devotional practices, including a form of meditation called *muraqaba*, the repetition of divine names and phrases, and ritualized prayer. The practice is perhaps best known for its poets, among them Rūmī and Hafiz, as well as the ecstatic sacred dances of the whirling dervishes.

A *tekke* is a gathering place for Sufis, a place of community and spiritual retreat. The Hala Sultan Tekke complex was built in phases between 1760 and 1817, during the Ottoman era, and contains the Mosque of Umm Haram, which is considered one of the holiest places in the Muslim world. Also on the site are a mausoleum, a minaret, and living quarters.

Care for the spirit

There is a Sufi saying, "Love the pitcher less and the water more." This bears contemplation, reminding us to be more concerned with our inner than our outer life, and with our spirit over the material world.

Although originally Muslim, Hala Sultan Tekke is now open to all, and nondenominational. The *tekke* is a stellar example of Ottoman architecture, but is also renowned for its myriad examples of calligraphy from various periods. It was built above the grave of Umm Haram, a follower and companion of Muhammad, believed to be the sister of the Prophet's foster mother.

Hala Sultan Tekke is set on the beautiful shores of the Larnaka, a salt lake. Local legend holds that the brininess of the flamingo-filled lake is the consequence of a selfish old woman denying the Christian saint Lazarus food and water. The water is so salty that when the lake evaporates in the summer, it forms a crust that eventually breaks down to create a gray haze.

Svatý Hostýn Cathedral and Healing Spring

Svatý (Holy) Hostýn, also called the Sanctuary of the Sacred Lady, is the most visited pilgrimage site in the Czech Republic. Stories tell how the site was built in gratitude to the Virgin Mary, and attribute special qualities to the holy water in its chapel. The historian and priest Bohuslav Balbín wrote in *Diva Montis Sancti* (1665) that during a raid on Moravia by the Turks in 1241 the local people sought sanctuary and prayed to Mary for help, and that a stream of clear water bubbled from the earth. Simultaneously, a huge storm arose with lightning so fierce that it forced the invaders to retreat. The first chapel was constructed there in 1544, and several more structures were built over the years, including the eighteenth-century basilica of the Assumption of the Virgin with its elegant dome and pair of towers.

Precious water

Water is a sacrament that spans all belief systems. Just as Christians use holy water for blessing and baptism, so do Buddhists, Muslims, Jews, Hindus, and practitioners of myriad Indigenous religions incorporate it into their rituals. Consider this the next time you drink water from a glass, wash your hands, or boil water for a pot of tea. Where did the water come from? How does it connect all of humanity and all of the planet?

Visitors can follow a special path as they recite prayers and honor the Stations of the Cross—locations marking the events of Jesus' Crucifixion. At each stop is a chapel, reflecting the folk architecture of Moravian Wallachia as well as Art Nouveau influences.

Hill of Crosses

Nobody knows the exact number of crosses on this hill near the town of Šiauliai in northern Lithuania, but it is estimated that there are well over 100,000. Most are inscribed with names, prayers, or supplications, and they span languages, nations, and religions. Some are left in gratitude, others request guidance, and some commemorate deaths or marriages or are placed to protect sports teams, travelers, or the sick.

Nobody is certain when pilgrims began placing crosses on this hill, but it is thought that the practice began after the Polish–Russian War in 1831. As time passed, it came to be a place in which to honor the peaceful fortitude of the Lithuanians throughout history. Soon, the devout also left crucifixes, statues of saints, rosaries, and handmade effigies.

The pilgrimage site became especially meaningful during the years of Soviet occupation from 1944 until 1990. Lithuanians visited the hill and left crosses and other tokens in solidarity and as a form of peaceful protest, despite the Soviets bulldozing the area several times. By the time the Lithuanians regained their independence, nearly 15,000 large crosses and more than 5,000 small crosses were counted there, a testament to hope and resilience.

What we leave behind

Although I am a believer in the adage "Leave nothing behind but your footprints," when it is appropriate, leaving things behind can unite people across borders and through time and space. Think of leaving a stone on a grave or flowers on someone's doorstep; more than a kind gesture, it can be an act of interconnectedness.

MALTESE ARCHIPELAGO

Filfla

If you sail around the southernmost point of Malta, you'll spot a rocky, uninhabited island. Filfla is tiny—less than half a square mile (1.3 sq. km)—which may be why many believe its name is derived from the Arabic word for peppercorn, *felfel-e*.

Filfla may have been holy ground for the earliest inhabitants of Malta, who built temples on the large islands nearby. A legend tells how God punished a Maltese village by causing the earth to swallow up the town and its evil inhabitants, directing angels to dump them all into the sea, which is how Filfla got its nickname Angel's Dump.

I am Filfla

The American author Emily A. Francis, who currently lives on Malta, shared this lovely meditation on Filfla with me:

I look like a rock out in the middle of the sea that no one is allowed to touch. Those who know me can feel my essence radiating strength and resilience as I stand proud with what remains after so much destruction passed over and through me. Dark hearts and bloody hands nearly destroyed half of me.

The other half held the chapel that was built into one of my caves. It was a place of salvation. Even after it was washed away, redemption remains. Prayers become purpose. Purpose becomes renewal.

Along with the bombs that were aimed at me, I hold the energy of all the prayers and contemplation of those who came before. Despite their attempts to break me down I'm still here. I am Filfla.

What is the name of the island that dwells deep within you?

The sole recorded permanent structure on Filfla is a chapel that was built in a cave in 1343 and destroyed in an earthquake in 1856. In the twentieth century, the British Royal Navy and Air Force used the island for target practice, and remnants of munitions, bullet casings, and perhaps unexploded ordnance are still scattered over the island. Happily, it became a bird reserve in 1980 and is now home to a variety of wildlife, including the endemic (living only there) Filfla wall lizard and the Maltese door snail.

Lake Baikal and Olkhon Island

Difficult to reach but worth the trip, Lake Baikal—also known as the Sacred Sea or the Pearl of Siberia—is a place of wonder. It is 25 million years old, the seventh largest lake on the planet—about the size of Belgium—and the deepest, reaching a depth of 5,000 ft (1,525 m) and containing 20 percent of the planet's fresh (and unfrozen) water, which surpasses the volume of all America's Great Lakes.

In part because the climate is so moderate there compared to the surrounding area—winter temperatures average -6°F (-21°C) and summer temperatures 52°F (11°C)—when it thaws in spring the lake is rife with flora and fauna. It is home to about 1,700 animal and plant species, out of which two-thirds—among them the Baikal seal, the world's only true freshwater seal—are endemic, which is why another name for it is the Galápagos of Russia. Baikal is one of the clearest lakes in the world, and its transparency contributes to this diversity because light reaches great depths, augmenting photosynthesis and thus plant life.

In 1675, the Moldavian writer, theologian, and explorer Nikolai Spathari described the remarkable ice floes: "The sea rests and is

divided in two, and there are cracks with the width of five meters [16 ft] or more, and the water from the lake does not spill over the ice but comes together again soon with great noise and thunder, and an ice shaft appears in that place; noise and great thunder persists everywhere under the ice of Lake Baikal in winter, as if someone (a great and fearless one) fires a cannon." The lake lies directly on the Baikal Rift Zone, so earthquakes are a regular occurrence—sometimes there are as many as 2,000 in a single year. Maybe that is the "someone (a great and fearless one)" that Spathari wrote about.

Throughout the lake are 27 islands. Perhaps the most remarkable is the largest, Olkhon, heavily forested with larch and pine, sparsely populated by humans but home to herds of wild horses. It is a sacred place for the Indigenous Buryat people, whose traditions imbue animals, forests, rivers, and even stones with life force.

North of the main settlement of Khuzhir, the dense forests become empty savannas and steppes. Trees are replaced by towering totems and piles of stones wrapped in brightly colored ribbons inscribed with prayers. The original inhabitants practiced a form of shamanism, which has merged with Buddhism over time. These totems can be found at intervals all the way north to the most sacred point on the island, Shamanka. Also called Shaman Rock, this is said to be the home of the deity Burkhan, where one is discouraged from thinking negative thoughts because they may upset the spirits.

Create a totem

There are various definitions of totem, but essentially they are objects (usually made from natural materials) that have some sort of sacred significance. Just as the large poles of Olkhon Island are considered a totem, so could be a Christmas tree or a small cairn or pile of stones. Create one for yourself, maybe from pebbles, seashells, or driftwood. You can adorn it with ribbons containing prayers or keep it simple, letting it be a reminder that every place is sacred if we choose to make it so.

The Way of St James

The cathedral of Santiago de Compostela in northwestern Spain is the reputed burial place of the Apostle St James the Great, and one of only three remaining churches to have been constructed over the tomb of an apostle. (The other two are St Peter's Basilica in the Vatican and the Cathedral of St Tomas in Chennai, India.) Since the Early Middle Ages, this cathedral—a Romanesque structure with Gothic and Baroque additions—and basilica have marked the end of the traditional pilgrimage route known as the Way of St James or the Camino de Santiago.

People began walking there as an act of devotion, penance, or even curiosity in the ninth century. It is said that the twelfth and thirteenth centuries were the "Golden Age" of pilgrimages to Santiago, and in 1492 Pope Alexander VI proclaimed the Camino de Santiago one of the "three great pilgrimages of Christendom."

Spiritual seekers of all religions have walked the Way of St James ever since, and more than 300,000 still do it each year. The journey starts at the pilgrim's home, but official routes begin in France, Portugal, and the Basque city of Irun, as well as other places as far away as North Africa. Part of the beauty of the process is the way it unifies the countries that are connected by the path. As they travel, pilgrims receive stamps in their "passports," culminating at the cathedral. Upon completing the pilgrimage they receive a *compostela* or certificate of accomplishment if they have met three conditions: made the trip out of religious conviction or in the mindset of spiritual search; traveled the last 62 miles (100 km) on foot or horseback or the last 124 miles (200 km) by bicycle; and collected a set of stamps in their passport.

Pilgrims can identify each other by the scallop-shell badges they wear. Over the years many meanings have been attributed to the symbol; perhaps it represents heaven or pilgrimage, but it may simply refer to the pilgrims' habit of bringing home shells from the nearby shores of the Atlantic or the Bay of Biscay as a souvenir.

Symbolism and iconography abound in the cathedral of St James, but a small detail merits notice. The south façade contains the Platerías door, from which the pilgrims depart after making the journey, and there the Greek symbol Chi-Rho appears between two arches. This early Christogram, which consists of the first two letters of Christ's name in Greek, is found in churches throughout the world, but what is interesting about this example is that the letters are backward. They remind us that the end becomes the beginning, and that the pilgrim is about to embark on the true spiritual journey back into their life.

Endings and beginnings

Just like the reversed Christogram, many endings in our lives are also beginnings. Compost becomes gardens, departures become arrivals, winter becomes spring.

DELPHI, GREECE

Temple of Apollo

You'll find the Temple of Apollo, known as "the navel of the world," in the complex of Delphi amid the cliffs of Mount Parnassus. It is said to be where Apollo—the god of the sun and of prophecy, and the son of Zeus—battled the huge serpent Python, the guardian of the mountain, thereby creating a place of divination. The location is said to have been chosen because of a fissure in the stone below it, which emitted vapors that induced a state of trance or delirium. Recent geological studies have confirmed the presence of light hydrocarbon gases—ethane, methane, and ethylene—in spring water nearby.

Delphic wisdom

Among the Delphic Maxims, five stood out for me:

> *As a child be well-behaved.*
> *As a youth be self-disciplined.*
> *As a middle-aged person be honest.*
> *As an old person be sensible.*
> *At your end be without sorrow.*

It is sage advice indeed. But what if you applied these to the cycle of your day as well as to your wider existence, building a life of moderation, discipline, honesty, balance, and ultimately joy?

Built on the site of an earlier temple or perhaps several, the existing shrine dates from the fourth century BCE. In ancient times the temple housed the high priestess known as the Delphic Oracle or the Pythia. Pilgrims and those who wished to consult the god Apollo through the Oracle first bathed in the waters of the Castalian Spring in a nearby ravine, as did the Pythia and her priests.

Inscribed throughout the temple are words of wisdom known as the 147 Delphic Maxims, likely created by the Seven Sages or Wise Men of Greece, a group of sixth-century philosophers, scholars, and statesmen, although they are sometimes attributed to Apollo via the Pythia. The maxims advise on a range of subjects. The three most famous ones are inscribed on a column in an entry area:

> *Know thyself.*
> *Nothing in excess,* or *Nothing overmuch.*
> *Surety brings ruin,* or *A pledge comes from madness.*

Sistine Chapel

The Vatican rivals Mecca as one of the most visited spiritual destinations on the planet, and the Sistine Chapel is one of its most sought-out spots. It is best known for its frescoes by Renaissance masters, including Botticelli and Perugino, but especially for those by Michelangelo, which some consider the greatest works of art created in the Western world.

Perhaps the best-known of these frescoes is *The Creation of Adam* (1508–12). The image of the hand of God—*primum movens* (the prime mover, the uncreated creator)—reaching to spark life into the hand of man is iconic. Over the years, the frescoes have been interpreted from a medical point of view, and biologists and doctors have analyzed them and taken into account Michelangelo's fascination with anatomy.

Obstetricians see the form surrounding the depiction of God as a postpartum uterus signifying actual birth, while nephrologists have interpreted the same image as kidneys.

An even more spectacular interpretation has been offered by the physician Frank Lynn Meshberger, who sees the shape of a human brain in the general

Find the divine spark

Regardless of your beliefs or whether you subscribe to Dr Meshberger's theory, there's a universality to seeking the mind of God, a collective self or divine spark that gives rise to the mortal self. Consider how the "marble spell" is broken and what *primum movens* means to you as you ponder your purpose in life.

forms. In 1990 he wrote: "In the fresco traditionally called the Creation of Adam … I believe that Michelangelo encoded a special message. It is a message consistent with thoughts he expressed in his sonnets. Supreme in sculpture and painting, he understood that his skill was in his brain and not in his hands. He believed that the 'divine part' we 'receive' from God is the 'intellect.'" Perhaps this was what Michelangelo was referring to in his fourteenth sonnet:

> *The best of artists hath no thought to show*
> *Which the rough stone in its superfluous shell*
> *Doth not include: to break the marble spell*
> *Is all the hand that serves the brain can do.*

Synagogue of Santa María la Blanca

The synagogue of Santa María la Blanca (St Mary the White) was originally known as the Ibn Shushan Synagogue, or the Congregational Synagogue of Toledo. This remarkable example of Moorish architecture has had many incarnations, and may be the oldest synagogue in Europe.

Pluralism—the condition in which two or more principles (in this case religions) coexist—has been the state of Santa María la Blanca since it was first built. It was constructed for Jewish worship, perhaps on the site of an existing mosque, by Islamic architects during the Middle Ages under the auspices of the Christian Kingdom of Castile, and is currently under the guardianship of the Catholic Church. It remains an emblem of the cooperation of the three Abrahamic religions on the Iberian Peninsula during this time, and illustrates why Toledo is often referred to as the City of Three Cultures.

The synagogue was converted to a church in the early fifteenth century and

Forever sacred

Santa María la Blanca has consistently remained a hallowed place. What are those places for you? Ones with layers of spiritual meaning? Holy by their own nature and beyond labels?

later named Santa María la Blanca after an altarpiece statue of the Virgin Mary in the building. In 2013, Toledo's Jewish community petitioned the city's Catholic archbishop to return the building to them. As a symbolic gesture, it was declared an historic monument, no longer the site of religious ceremonies, but a museum for all.

Shrine of the Black Madonna

From a white Madonna in Spain to a black one in Croatia … Marija Bistrica contains the largest shrine to the Virgin Mary in Croatia, and dates back to the start of the thirteenth century. This architecturally impressive pilgrimage site includes a church, a convent for cloistered Carmelite nuns, and inspiring Stations of the Cross—14 places for prayer and devotion—sculpted by various Croatian artists.

Consider your essential nature

Although some representations of the Madonna were brown or black originally, others have grown darker over time, as smoke from candles and incense has accumulated. The Swiss psychoanalyst Carl Jung wrote about the archetype of a black Madonna, seeing it as a symbol of the depth of the feminine spirit, from Mary to the Egyptian goddess Isis, who healed the sick and guided the dead into the afterlife. A connection could also be made to many goddesses such as the Greek Demeter, Hindu Kali, or Buddhist Tara. The Jungian analyst Ean Begg elaborated on this idea in *The Cult of the Black Virgin* (1985): "Underneath all our conditioning, hidden in the crypt of our being … the Black Virgin is enthroned with her Child, the dark latency of our own essential nature, that which we were always meant to be."

Consider this notion in terms of your whole being. What is your essential nature or the soul that you were always meant to be?

   Marija Bistrica is best known for the statue after which it is named. This Madonna, painted black, was created in 1499 by an anonymous artist and placed in a chapel within the shrine complex. Half a century later, when the Turks invaded, a local priest hid it in the church wall beneath a stained-glass window. It was rediscovered in 1588, only to be hidden and recovered yet again in the mid-seventeenth century. In 1882, a new church in the complex was completed, but a fire destroyed the entire church, except the altar and the statue, leading believers to deem it a miracle. The church was rebuilt in 1923, and in 1935 the archbishop of Zagreb crowned the black Madonna Queen of Croatia—a name it still holds today.

Thingvellir National Park

This area was originally called Bláskógar (Blue Woods) because of the many birch trees that once flourished there. Breathtaking landscapes, hot springs, icy cascades of lava-filtered water, the northern lights, and Iceland's largest lake— the startlingly clear Thingvallavatn— all are in this active volcanic region on the Mid-Atlantic Ridge, which separates the tectonic plates of the Eurasian and North American continents. It is no surprise that it is often described as the spiritual heart of Iceland, and for millennia, Norse, Celtic, and Christian gods have been worshipped on this site.

Thingvellir (which can be translated as "assembly plains") contains the remains of the place where all the tribes of Iceland assembled regularly between the years 930 and 1798, forming the Althing—what many call the world's first parliament. The eleventh-century Icelandic

Thingvellir National Park 47

Meaningful places

What a privilege to have access to a location like this! It is worth wondering how we can find such places of meaning and community in our own lives. They may not have crystalline lakes or be at the intersection of continents, but parks, religious centers, even libraries can serve this purpose.

sagas describe people from across the country congregating there to make decisions and navigate their nation's course. Although no longer an official place of government, it is still a symbol of Icelandic unity and respect for "natural" and "noble" laws.

Yet it is the magnificence of this landscape—which has remained largely unchanged since the tenth century—that makes it spiritual and draws seekers today. Many writers have likened Thingvellir to a sanctuary or church, a place of ritual and sacrament that goes beyond religion or political position, a place for gathering to experience the wonders of nature. In 1907, when few people in the world were thinking about the preservation of nature, the historian Matthías Þórðarson (who also conceived the design of the Icelandic flag) wrote an article called "Protection of Beautiful Places and Remarkable Natural Phenomena." In it he considered the importance of conserving areas that were meaningful and extraordinary solely for their natural beauty. He believed this was just as important as protecting archaeological discoveries and religious objects, perhaps more so, and suggested Thingvellir as one such sacred site.

herding these creatures in the seventeenth century, traveling in groups of humans and herds called *sildat*. Now, although Sámi lives tend to be less nomadic, the reindeer are no less important. During periods when the Sámi were forced by the dominant cultures to assimilate, reindeer herding was a way for them to sustain their heritage and even their language. Now, in Sweden and Norway, Sámi reindeer husbandry is officially protected.

Kamppi Chapel of Silence

A bustling shopping center in the heart of a major city might not seem the most spiritual of places, but the Kamppi Chapel of Silence is just that. This ecumenical chapel, which looks a bit like a windowless but elegant alien spacecraft, is not used for religious services or events such as weddings, but rather was constructed for a single and specific purpose: individual calm, quiet, and reflection.

The Finnish proverb "Talking is silver; silence is gold" reflects a cultural way of being that is embodied in the nation's habits, from hikes in the many dense, hushed forests to the socially acceptable long (two- or three-minute) pauses in conversations, even during business meetings. So when Finland set out to become more of a destination for tourists, it created a delegation to explore the country's marketable qualities. Landscape, education, and renowned design were all considered, but what they landed on was something entirely different: silence. This is a quality that Finns value,

especially as technology and media make our world increasingly loud. The Finnish Tourist Board announced that "In the future, people will be prepared to pay for the experience of silence."

Much of the chapel is built from the wood of alder, a tree that is ubiquitous in this, the

most forested country in Europe. Will the silence of the chapel perhaps inspire you to venture into the woods?

A moment of quiet

Stop for a moment. Stop making noise. Stop wanting stuff. Stop trying to control things. Stop attempting to undo the done. Be quiet. Truly. Breathe in silence. Exhale clarity. And in your own chapel of silence, practice as the Chan Buddhism teacher Rebecca Li suggests: *Stay with this just as this. Stay with that just as that.*

Sultan Ahmed Mosque

Although there are a few "blue mosques" in the Muslim world, the Ottoman one constructed in Istanbul in the seventeenth century, commissioned during the rule of Sultan Ahmed I and built by the famed architect Mehmed Āghā, is one of the most remarkable. This is in no small part because the ceiling is set with over 20,000 bright blue tiles, covering more than three-quarters of the mosque's surface area.

The grandeur doesn't end there. The mosque is illuminated by more than 200 stained-glass windows, supplemented by chandeliers. Incorporated into each golden chandelier is an ostrich eggshell that repels spiders and saves the caretakers from having to clean the cobwebs. (This delights me, and it shows there's more than one way to honor a sacred space.) Even the floors express the sanctity of the mosque, being carpeted in rugs that have been donated by the faithful over generations.

In the Muslim world the color blue represents the heavens and has divine

Showing respect

If you look at the main gate at the north entrance of the mosque, you will notice a pair of symbolic chains hanging down. These were placed to encourage everyone—even a sultan arriving on horseback—to bow down upon entering. This may seem archaic; why bow to a place? But think about the gesture: it's the embodiment of the recognition of the sacred, the fact that one is about to enter hallowed ground.

implications, reminding us to reflect on what is holy. A study of color in Islamic architecture by the Iranian architecture professor J. Mahdi Nejad confirms that blue is a symbol of spirituality and faith: "Blue is the color of stillness and balance … Blue is a clear and bright color, fresh and calm, sweet, quiet, surrendered, and primarily blue is a holy color and sacred in the Islamic culture, because it is the color of sky where God, pure souls, and angels are."

CHAPTER 2

MIDDLE EAST
AND AFRICA

ABU SIMBEL
Aswan Governorate, Egypt

Moulay Idriss Zerhoun

Near the better-known cities of Fez and Meknes, Moulay Idriss Zerhoun is often referred to as the holiest city in Morocco, second only to Mecca as a place of pilgrimage. Composed primarily of hundreds of whitewashed buildings spread over two hills at the foot of Mount Zerhoun, the vista of this settlement evokes the mystical.

When it first opened up to Western visitors, the novelist Edith Wharton described Moulay Idriss in her travelogue *In Morocco* (1920): "Below the plateau, the land drops down precipitately to a narrow river-valley green with orchards and gardens, and in the neck of the valley, where the hills meet again, the conical white

The call to prayer

One of the beautiful things about spending time in predominantly Muslim countries or neighborhoods is hearing the call to prayer sung from minarets or broadcast via loudspeakers by *muezzins* five times a day. It proclaims the greatness of God and urges the faithful to *Hayya 'ala-s-Salah*—hurry to prayer. People will often stop where they are, unfold prayer rugs, and begin to pray, or head to a nearby mosque. The Arabic term for this summoning is *adhan*, a word that comes from *adhina*, which means "to be attentive, to listen, to hear."

This is a profound ritual that could radically shift our lives. Imagine if we made it a point of urgency to be attentive to that which is holy five times a day, to say a prayer, or just pause and be present.

town of Moulay Idriss, the Sacred City of Morocco, rises sharply against a wooded background … there is surely not another town in North Africa as white as Moulay Idris … But Moulay Idriss, that afternoon, was as white as if its arcaded square had been scooped out of a big cream cheese."

The city is the site of the mosque and burial place of Idris I (745–791 CE), the first major Islamic Moroccan ruler and a direct descendent of the Prophet Muhammad, and it is this that makes the city and sanctuary so holy. Sometimes called a Muslim saint, Idris was both a political and a religious leader, and is now revered as Morocco's *wali* or spiritual protector.

Caves of Tassili n'Ajjer

One of the most important groupings of prehistoric cave art in the world, and the oldest in the Sahara, is found in Tassili n'Ajjer National Park, near the border with Libya and Niger. The park spans an area of more than 28,000 sq. miles (72,520 sq. km)—more than 40 times the size of London.

In this orange moonscape, amid the caves and eroded sandstone "forests of rock," are more than 15,000 drawings and engravings dating from 6000 BCE to the first centuries CE. The images are clearly primitive, yet also strangely modern, depicting groups of people hunting, farming, and engaging in rituals, as well as myriad fauna and various animals, including giraffes, camels, and horses. They constitute a record of shifts in climate, the migration of animals, and human cultural evolution over the span of their creation.

In addition to aesthetic and historical interest, these images have a lot to teach us about climate change. For example, images of hippopotamuses, which have been extinct in this region for thousands of years, imply the former existence of a major water source, and the depictions of farming allude to a time before the landscape

Impermanence

Sit with the truth of impermanence and contrast it with the untruth of permanence. A lake becomes a desert … a seed a baobab, lemon, or yew … a baby a grandparent. Nothing remains what it is.

became desert. For me, such profound evidence of the cycles and scope of life shows the extent to which we assume the permanence of things that may be fleeting, and that makes it a sacred place. We are each a tiny ephemeral piece of the eternal cosmic puzzle.

Ancient City of Petra

"The loftiest portals ever raised by the hands of man, the proudest monuments of architectural skill and daring, sink into insignificance by the comparison." That's how the American explorer and archaeologist John Lloyd Stephens described the approach to Petra through the narrow winding crevasse called Al Siq in *Incidents of Travel in Egypt, Arabia Petraea, and the Holy Land* (1835). Located in Jordan's southwestern desert and dating back to the third century BCE, Petra was the capital of the lost ancient Nabataean Kingdom, which spanned the Arabian and Sinai peninsulas from the fourth century BCE to the first century CE. It contains temples and tombs carved directly into the glowing, red-pink sandstone cliffs, earning it its nickname, the "Rose City."

As a stopping point between the Red Sea and the Dead Sea, Petra was an important crossroads in the Arabian trade routes. Legend suggests that it is where Moses struck a rock with his rod, releasing water to assuage the Israelites' thirst, and it contains the mosque on the peak of Jebel Haroun, the traditional burial place of the prophet

Wonder of the world

Imagine the marvel of Petra, of passing through a crevasse in the stone and emerging into an unexpected, grand landscape. It is no surprise that Stephens described it as "the most wonderful object in the world." Don't lose sight of the world's wonders. What brings you delight?

Aaron. In this remarkable city there is also a monastery, an amphitheater, many tombs, colonnades, gardens, baths, and marketplaces, all carved from the same sandstone. It is a fantastical blend of Assyrian and Hellenistic architecture, from Neolithic to Byzantine. Not only is it a remarkable feat of construction with reservoirs, aqueducts, and cisterns to conserve rainfall, but it also has a mythical quality that captures and stirs the imagination.

KONYA, TURKEY

Mevlâna Museum

The Mevlâna Museum is the location of the mausoleum of the thirteenth-century Persian Sufi mystic, Islamic scholar, philosopher, and arguably most beloved poet on the planet, Jalāl al-Dīn Rūmī, who was born in Afghanistan but died in Konya. The tomb's beauty is a fitting tribute, and the universality of his wisdom, reflected by his epitaph, is what makes this place sacred: "When we are dead, seek not our tomb in the earth, but find it in the hearts of men."

The area was also once a lodge for the Mevlevi or "whirling dervish" order of Sufism, founded by early followers of Rūmī. They are best known for their dances which are an ecstatic connection to God and a way to meld poetry, movement, and spirit. Like the dervishes' dances, Rūmī's writing embodies the presence of God as the Beloved.

Spiritual words

Reading the poetry of Rūmī could be seen as a spiritual practice in itself. Here is some of his writing to ponder when considering spiritual spaces, thin places, and what makes a destination sacred:

> I looked around, and saw in all Heaven's Spaces: One!
> In Ocean's rippling Waves and billowy Races: One!
> I looked into the Heart, and saw a Sea, wide Worlds
> All full of Dreams, and in all Dreaming Faces: One!
> Thou art the First, the Last, the Outer, Inner, Whole:
> Thy Light breaks through in all Earth's Hues and Graces: One!
> Thou seest All from East to furthest Bound of West,
> And lo! each Leaf and Flower and Tree Crown traces: One!
> Four wild and restive Steeds draw on the World's vast Car;
> Thou bridlest them, and rul'st in all their Paces: One!
> Air, Fire, Earth, Water melt to One in Fear of thee;
> Nor struggle wild, but show in close Embraces: One!
> The Hearts of all that live in Earth and Heav'n above,
> Beat Praise to thee; nor fails in all their Places—One.

Rock-Hewn Churches

Near a traditional village in the mountains of Ethiopia, in an area that is sometimes called New Jerusalem, are 11 thirteenth-century cave churches described as "prayer in stone." This is not a huge surprise, since Ethiopia became a hub of Christianity after the faith took root there in the early fourth century, but what is unusual is the way these medieval churches were constructed: hewn out of the bedrock. Columns, windows, plumbing, and other architectural elements were added later to the red stone of these remarkable buildings. Some of the churches contain corridors for ceremonial processions, and others passageways to catacombs and hermit caves.

The churches were built in two groups, divided by the River Jordan: five houses to the south and five houses to the north. An eleventh structure—the House of St George, which is built in the shape of a cross—is separate from the others.

King Gebre Meskel Lalibela, who was later venerated as a saint, is credited with sponsoring the construction of the churches after the Muslim conquests made travel to Jerusalem in Palestine more difficult. Said to have been instructed by God to create something humans had never before seen, King Lalibela built his own Jerusalem, and soon thereafter Christians began to make pilgrimages there. They still do, particularly members of the Ethiopian Orthodox Christian Church, for whom this remains an active place of worship—so much so that of the 6,000 inhabitants of the surrounding village, 1,500 are priests.

The music within you

The style of Ethiopian Christian liturgical chant known as Zema has been practiced since the sixth century and is traditionally identified with a composer who also created the Ethiopian system of musical notation, which is mnemonic and represents pitch or melody. Zema is presented at church services and on holy days, its resonant, fluid sound interwoven with sacrament.

Sometimes it is a piece of music, sometimes it is a poem, but each of us has embodied certain verses and stanzas that are more than language and that resonate within us. What are yours?

Abu Simbel

Seeing Abu Simbel for the first time evokes the colossal grandeur that we tend to associate with ancient Egypt. This complex near the border with Sudan was built during the thirteenth century BCE to commemorate Pharaoh Ramses II's triumph at the Battle of Kadesh. To give a sense of the magnificence of its scale, the four colossal figures of Ramses are about 66 ft (20 m) tall. Covering 262 sq. miles (679 sq. km), the complex includes two rock-hewn temples—one dedicated to the deities Ra, Ptah, and Amun, as well as Ramses, with iconic statues of 32 ft (10 m) in height dominating the façade, and a smaller temple dedicated to the pharaoh's most beloved wife, Nefertari, and also to Hathor, the goddess of love, fertility, and the sky.

As literally monumental as Abu Simbel is, it was lost (at least to Europeans) for a considerable period. It fell into disuse around the sixth century BCE and was forgotten, partially buried in sand, until the Swiss writer and traveler Johann Ludwig Burckhardt rediscovered it in 1813. Burkhardt shared the news with his fellow explorer Giovanni Battista Belzoni, who ultimately excavated the temples and statues. Carl Jung spoke about it in a seminar in the 1930s: "The stone speaks … an antique Egyptian temple is a most marvelous example of what stone can say … It grows out of stone— the temple of Abu Simbel, for example, is amazing in that respect."

Although the colossi of Abu Simbel appear to have grown from the stone, as often happens with growing things, they were in fact transplanted. In a remarkable feat of architectural engineering, the entire temple complex was disassembled and relocated in 1968 so

that it wouldn't be submerged in Lake Nasser, the reservoir formed by the construction of the Aswan Dam. It was a financial effort as well, costing the equivalent of $300 million today to cut and move each block of stone, averaging about 20 tons apiece. As you approach Abu Simbel by airplane today it would never occur to you that it hadn't always been there exactly as it is.

The collective unconscious

Picking a place in Egypt felt almost impossible. My parents spent a couple months every year there during much of my youth, and when I finally got an opportunity to visit, I'd seen so many slide shows (those were the days before Instagram) and heard so many stories that it was almost as if I were returning to a place I knew. But maybe all ancient places are like that for everyone—even without the souvenirs and long-awaited postcards. Perhaps this is what Jung was referring to in 1934 when he wrote about that "deeper layer, which does not derive from personal experience and is not a personal acquisition but is inborn. This deeper layer I call the 'collective unconscious.' I have chosen the term 'collective' because this part of the unconscious is not individual but universal; in contrast to the personal psyche, it has contents and modes of behavior that are more or less the same everywhere and in all individuals." In this we're like the colossi at Abu Simbel: born, lost to our shadows or journeys, and reborn into another version of ourselves that is wholly the same yet not.

Lake Fundudzi

This site is sacred to the Vhatavhatsindi, or People of the Pool, part of the Indigenous Bantu VhaVenda people. It is recommended that travelers address the lake in the traditional manner—*ukodola*—to prevent bad luck befalling them. To do this, face away from the lake, bend, and look at the water through your legs. If you would like to receive even more blessings, walk to the water's edge and toss in a strand or two of your hair.

Although three rivers run into Lake Fundudzi, it never overflows. This is said to be because the lake is watched over by a python god. After washing in the lake, he beats his large stone drums. Residents celebrate him every year with the *domba*, or Python Dance, performed by adolescent girls from nearby villages. It is said that the lake's color reflects the mood of the ancestors and will predict the abundance or lack of precipitation in the coming rainy season.

The power of rituals

Rituals such as *ukodola* connect humanity to a particular place over millennia and weave a path to the sacred. Look at rituals in your life: perhaps the way a parent or grandparent offered a prayer, set a table for a holiday meal, or uttered a phrase to ward off the evil eye. See what happens when you reincorporate such rituals in your life.

Kuumbi Cave

In Swahili, the Kuumbi Cave is called Pango la Luumbi, meaning the "Cave of Creation." This vast limestone cave is on the southeastern coast of Unguja Island, in the Indian Ocean. Part of a coral reef, it was first inhabited more than 20,000 years ago and continued to be until the early to mid-twentieth century, when the residents moved to nearby villages.

Conservationists and archaeologists are working to preserve the site's cultural heritage, which, along with the surrounding forest, is considered sacred by the local population and still used for weekly rituals and worship.

The geology and natural history of the cave are remarkable, too. If you venture in you will encounter stalactites, stalagmites, vast limestone formations, and even a subterranean lake. The community living near the cave believes that spirits of the ancestors (Mizmu) dwell in its darkest depths, which is a sensible conclusion since many of the residents are likely direct descendants of people buried there.

There is abundant animal life in the area, but especially interesting is the Zanzibar leopard, which is said to hide in the caves. It was once the area's apex predator, but was believed to be extinct. However, in 2018, a leopard was recorded by conservationists on a camera trap, reviving hope for the species.

Connection to ancestors

For me, the spiritual thrill of Kuumbi is the continuity. Elderly residents of the nearby town of Jambiani clearly recall their grandparents and great-grandparents living in the cave as hunter-gatherers—just as their ancestors had 20,000 years ago. Imagine the power of being so directly connected to how your predecessors lived. It's astounding.

CHAPTER 3

ASIA AND AUSTRALASIA

MOUNT HUANGSHAN
Anhui Province, China

Caves of Ellora

The more than one hundred Caves of Ellora are actually not natural caves at all; they make up the largest rock-cut temple complex in the world. Carved from the vertical face of the Charanandri Hills, primarily during the fifth to tenth centuries, they feature Hindu temples and monasteries, but also include Buddhist and Jain structures in a testament to the relative religious accord during this period of India's history.

In an article in *The New York Times* in October 1988, the anthropologist Moana Tregaskis described the experience of the Kailasa Cave, cave 16, named after the holy Mount Kailash: "Pavilion, assembly hall, vestibule, sanctuary, tower, courtyard, and gateway were hand chiseled out of one solid rock, freed from the hill on all four sides and, in the ultimate achievement of rock cutting, the ceiling was cut away. Twice the area of the Parthenon and one and a half times

as high, the Kailasa is the crowning achievement of eighth- and early ninth-century rock cutting." Within this tribute to the god Shiva is a spire shaped like Mount Kailash, panels depicting Hindu epics, and shrines dedicated to Krishna, Ganga, Yamuna, Saraswati, Vishnu, Vedic gods, and more.

Most of the Buddhist caves are more monastery than temple, with prayer halls, living quarters, and meditation niches, all adorned with shrines and carvings. The Jain caves are at the northern end and are smaller than the others, but equally detailed, depicting the 24 Jinas—human beings who have attained Enlightenment and spread the Jain principle that spiritual progress and freedom from suffering are the responsibility of all.

Chanting for Enlightenment

Cave 10, the Vīśvakarmā Cave, is renowned for its acoustics. Buddhist psychologist, meditation teacher, and pilgrimage guide Dr Miles Neale has chanted there, most often reciting the chant "Om Muni Muni Mahamuni Shakyamuni Soha," a mantra which is said to carry the energy of the Buddha's Enlightenment in its very syllables. Try chanting it yourself: inhale deeply and exhale each phrase from your core, with purpose, as if drawing from and connecting with all that is meaningful.

Birthplace of the Buddha

It is said that in about 563 BCE, as Queen Māyā of Sakya prepared to give birth, she traveled to Lumbini, near Kapilavastu. There she bathed in a holy pond, and in a garden, while holding on to a branch of a *sal* tree, she delivered her son Prince Siddhartha Gautama. Not only was the birth said to be pain-free and pure, but also, remarkably, the newborn baby immediately took seven steps as a lotus flower emerged to mark each one. Seven days after that, the queen died.

The city of Lumbini celebrates this event with its many temples, monuments, and monasteries, and a museum. Pilgrims from around the world come to meditate and chant at the site of the holy birth from dawn until dusk. The garden has been developed into a bird sanctuary, and is now home to nearly 300 pairs of sarus cranes.

Thirty-five years after his birth, Māyā's son sat down under a fig tree about 250 miles (400 km) away, in what is now Bodh Gaya in the Indian state of Bihar. He found Enlightenment as he realized the true nature of things, and became what we now call the Buddha, founder of one of the largest and most influential religions in the world. At the end of his ministry, as he was dying, he asked his companion and disciple Ananda to make him a bed between two *sal* trees, connecting to his first moments with his mother. Upon his death, like the lotus flowers eight decades earlier, the *sal* trees burst into spontaneous bloom, scattering their petals over his body.

Every birth has potential

Stephen Batchelor, a Buddhist scholar and teacher, writes on his website: "The birth of the Buddha shows that each child that is born has the same potential as the Buddha, the same possibility to awaken, to be wise and compassionate. Can we encounter each child as the Buddha himself? Can we see in each person the potential for wisdom and compassion?" Consider how every birth can redirect the course of history.

Golden Temple
or Harmandir Sahib

Amritsar means "Pool of the Nectar of Immortality," and was the site of a sacred pool used for centuries as a place of meditation by pilgrims and priests, and reportedly even by the Buddha himself. It was also visited by Guru Nanak, who founded Sikhism in the early sixteenth century as a faith distinct from Hinduism and Islam and rooted in his conviction in equality for all humans, regardless of gender, belief system, caste, or any other difference. Consequently, the pool became a shrine sacred to Nanak's disciples.

Over time, the pool was developed into a lake and a temple complex grew up under the oversight of Guru Nanak's nine successors. Guru Arjan Sahib, the Fifth Guru, conceived the idea of a central place of worship for Sikhs and drafted plans for a temple which was built in 1604. After founding the Sikh Empire in 1830, to embody the Sikh message of *ik onkar* or "one God," Maharaja Ranjit Singh rebuilt the temple in marble and copper and overlaid the shrine with gold foil, leading to the name of the Golden Temple.

The temple is now open to all worshippers, regardless of faith or origin. Rituals carried out there include chanting scripture, lighting candles, and walking around the lake, as well as the Sikh tradition of feeding the hungry without discrimination.

Accept blessings

Near the pool is a 400-year-old *ber* or Indian plum tree called Dukh
Bhanjani and known familiarly as "suffering remover." Sikh devotees
do not pick the fruit, but rather sit under it in the hopes it will fall on
them and imbue them with its blessings. This practice makes me
think of the Second Buddhist precept: refrain from taking what is not
given; accept what is freely offered. We can apply this concept in our
lives, since blessings tend to come when we're not grasping for them.

Ganges River

The Ganges River, or River of Heaven, is sacred to Hindus and to all people of India. Also known as the Mother Ganges, it is personified as the goddess Ganga, who, as she was born from Brahma the Creator's water vessel, was tangled in the god Shiva's hair, which he then shook down onto the Earth, allowing her to fall as the sacred river. It flows from a glacier cave high in the western Himalayas, through northern India and Bangladesh, before emptying into the Bay of Bengal. It sustains more than 10 percent of the Earth's population during this journey of 1,569 miles (2,525 km).

There's a passage from the Upanishads—the sacred Hindu texts—which reads: "The world is the river of god, flowing from Him and flowing back to Him." Like Shiva's tangled hair, the river is intertwined with all who are near it. It is seen as a force of order

The power of words

As the seventeenth-century poet and Sanskrit scholar Jagannatha put it in his devotional poem to the river, the "Ganga Lahiri": "If it is sung it immediately removes the worldly torment and sin. May this word 'Ganga' which is indeed pleasant to hear shine in my lotus-like mouth at the very end of my breath." Words have power to evoke, to heal, and to grant peace. Think about mantras and prayers, and how repetition provides solace or grounding. What words help you?

in a world of disorder, so much so that the devout travel there to take a sip of her water upon death. The Ganges is believed to have the power to cleanse sin which is so strong that a single drop carried on a breeze can purify the sins of many lifetimes. It is said that even merely thinking about the river can purify your soul.

Mount Huangshan

Mount Huangshan is actually a mountain range made up of many peaks, the tallest being Lotus Peak, Bright Peak, and Celestial or "Capital of Heaven" Peak. It spans almost 60 sq. miles (155 sq. km). Reflecting its origin in the movement of glaciers millions of years ago, the landscape is rugged, and renowned for its spectacular sunrises and a halo-like optical phenomenon called Buddha's Light created by moonlight interacting with mist and clouds.

Many of the Huangshan pine trees that grow straight out of the rocks are more than 100 years old, and one, the treasured "Welcoming Guests Pine," is said to be more than 1,500 years old. Taoists and Buddhists clearly felt welcomed to this place, since they each built temples and monasteries throughout the mountain range.

Let nature inspire you

The mighty mountain peaks that seem to pierce this "Sea of Clouds" are the stuff of myriad paintings and literature, contributing to yet another name for Huangshan: the Mountain of 20,000 Poems. Li Bai (701–762 CE)—who is regarded by many as the greatest poet in Chinese history—was deeply inspired by Mount Huangshan.

Sit quietly for a few moments in nature and let it inspire you. What songs do you hear? How does the breeze feel on your skin? Where does your mind go?

DATONG, SHANXI PROVINCE, CHINA

Yungang Grottoes

The Yungang Grottoes in the valley of the Shi Li River are comprised of over 1,000 caves and niches containing more than 51,000 statues of the Buddha, bodhisattvas, and other Enlightened beings in less than 1½ sq. miles (4 sq. km). They are a remarkable example of fifth- and sixth-century carving and cave art.

Perhaps most famous are the five caves commissioned in the fifth century by Emperor Wencheng under the direction of the monk

Repetition as ritual

I feel that power comes not only from the beauty of the artwork, but also from the sheer surge of repetition in the extraordinary number of statues to be seen at Yungang. It is something that can play into all our lives in the form of ritual. Repeating an act—a prayer, a mantra, a simple offering—myriad times imbues it not just with loveliness but also with the essence of the eternal reality or our deepest truth.

Tan Yao. They are considered the epitome of Chinese classical art, and of them, three are especially compelling. Cave 20 holds a colossal seated Buddha, 42 ft (13 m) long, in a meditation posture. Cave 6 depicts scenes from the Buddha's life story: his birth, departing his princely kingdom, awakening to his first sermon at the Deer Park, and ultimate nirvana. A lesser cave, 19, opened recently and immediately became a favorite. Along with about 4,000 smaller Buddha statues, it contains a poignant (and mammoth) statue of the Buddha tenderly patting the head of his son Rahula as he meets him for the first time after his journey of Enlightenment.

Paro Taktsang Monastery

Paro Taktsang—the "Tiger's Nest"—is smaller than most monastery complexes. It is a group of buildings perched on the edge of a cliff, almost 3,000 ft (900 m) above the Paro Valley, and its precarious situation contributes to the magic of this Himalayan Buddhist site.

Padmasambhava (Born from a Lotus), or Guru Rinpoche (Precious Guru), was a Buddhist master from India. He is credited for bringing Buddhism to Bhutan and elsewhere—specifically Vajrayana Buddhism, or the Diamond way, the third major Buddhist path, generally referred to when speaking of Tibetan Buddhism.

At Paro Taktsang, four temple buildings were built around eight caves. Among them, the "Shrine of the Guru with Eight Names," honors Padmasambhava's eight manifestations—the forms in which he incarnated on Earth. The name Tiger's Nest comes from the

Revealing what is hidden

It is said that Padmasambhava and Yeshe Tsogyal hid several holy texts or ritual objects near the Tiger's Nest, to be discovered by spiritual treasure-finders. A collection of sacred texts including the Tibetan Book of the Dead was one such treasure, recovered in the fourteenth century. However, many believe that what is hidden is not the physical text, but rather the wisdom in the mind of the spiritual teacher. Who or what are the revealers in your life? Much of a spiritual journey involves looking for the things that are hidden, unseen.

legend that Padmasambhava flew on the back of the Enlightened Yeshe Tsogyal (also known as the Mother of Tibetan Buddhism), whom he transformed into a tigress. Upon his arrival in Bhutan, Padmasambhava meditated for three weeks, three days, and three hours, and then tamed demons in the Paro Valley.

Shrine of Hazrat Shah Jalal

The Shah Jalal Shrine or *dargah* is the largest and most visited pilgrimage destination in Bangladesh. It is the burial place of the fourteenth-century Sufi saint and Muslim hero Shah Jalal, "the patron saint of Sylhet," who is credited with spreading Islam in the region. He was a Hafiz (a person who has committed the entire Qur'an to memory), and achieved Kamaliyat (spiritual perfection) after three decades of meditation and study.

It is said that Shah Jalal's uncle gave him a handful of soil and told him to journey through India until he found a place where the soil was the same color and composition. There, he should teach about Islam. Shah Jalal spent years traveling throughout the Indian subcontinent, spreading the teachings of Islam.

Originally constructed in the mid-sixteenth century, the complex has been added to over the centuries. Several

Connecting with the departed

I find Shah Jalal compelling: the earnest young missionary with a handful of earth in his pocket, looking to share the wisdom that meant so much to him. I'm also drawn to the legacy of his birds and how, even when we've passed on, we can connect with those we've left behind through animals, plants, or a powerful memory. Think about departed loved ones and how they might connect with you—or you with them.

mosques have been built around Shah Jalal's burial place, as well as a religious school and a cemetery. Shah Jalal's swords, Qur'an, prayer rug, cups, and bowls are also housed there. Opposite the tomb is a Langar Khana, a kitchen built to feed the hungry. To the west of the tomb is a well called Chashma, which, according to local lore, Shah Jalal instructed to be dug. The water from it is considered holy.

The shrine's water reservoir is also the stuff of legend. Catfish and snakehead fish called *gozar* are kept there, and feeding them is a popular tourist activity. It is said that they are fallen soldiers cursed by the shah to spend eternity as fish, although a gentler version of the story says they are descendants of pet fish bred by the shah. And with fish come birds; the blue rock pigeons that are plentiful in the area are called *jalali kobutor*, meaning "Jalal's pigeons." They're protected and encouraged to breed, and it is believed that they are descended from a pair he received as a gift.

Mahamuni Temple

Legend has it that the Buddha could travel through time and space, a feat so magical that he immediately converted King Chandra-surya and his court to Buddhism. They requested an image to honor, so the Buddha rallied the gods themselves to craft a likeness of himself. This likeness, said to be one of only five made during his lifetime, was called the Mahamuni, or "Great Sage." The Buddha was so delighted by the gods' handiwork that he breathed on the statue and charged it with magical powers. The statue rose and made a gesture of welcome, as the Buddha prophesied that it would exist for 5,000 years and help to save both humans and spirits. And powers it had, although they gradually began to fade as the years ticked away.

Daily devotion

The Vietnamese Zen master Thich Nhat Hanh has often likened washing the dishes to bathing a newborn baby Buddha, to illustrate how the profane is sacred and "Everyday mind is Buddha mind." I believe that's the lesson the monks are sharing as they wash the face of the Buddha's statue each day. We'd all benefit from approaching every act—be it housecleaning, a conference call, a train ride, or working in our garden—as an act of devotion, by being mindful, attentive, and fully in the process.

The Mahamuni Temple, often described as the most important religious site in Mandalay, was built in the early nineteenth century by King Bodawpaya to house the Mahamuni. Since this statue is considered an object of devotion, the architecture of the temple is secondary to the importance of the icon. The building is seven stories tall and has 253 gilded pillars mirrored with glass. When a fire broke out in the temple in the late nineteenth century, despite much of the building being spared, so much melted gold was recovered that craftsmen used it to fashion a new robe for the statue.

This 6-ft-high (2-m) golden Buddha is now kept in a small chamber, where it sits on a throne making a gesture that represents the dissolution of death, rebirth, and desire. Every morning at dawn, the monks of the temple perform an elaborate hour-long ritual that includes brushing the statue's teeth, washing its face, and polishing it with fresh towels. It is then rubbed with scented sandalwood paste, buffed again, and sprinkled with perfumed water. The used towels are given away for use on devotees' home altars and shrines.

SIEM REAP, CAMBODIA

Angkor Wat

A holy city deep in the Cambodian jungle, Angkor Wat (City of Temples) is the largest religious structure and one of the most important Buddhist pilgrimage sites on our planet. Arriving there is like emerging from the jungle in a fairytale, but instead of a secret garden, it is a secret city. Secret, but not small: its 38 sq. miles (100 sq. km) contain temples, shrines, houses, and waterways. In its heyday it accommodated 500,000 people—picture that! The

Awe and wonder

Angkor Wat is considered one of the wonders of the world. And wonder, as well as its companion, awe, is something we all need more of in our lives. Angkor Wat inspires both because, despite all we now know about the history and architecture of the holy city, it remains a mysterious place. Seek out wonder in your days and awe in your quiet moments, and look for the paths of presence and insight this can inspire.

panorama is dominated by four mammoth lotus bud-shaped towers surrounding a 213-ft (65-m) spire that aligns with the morning sun of the spring equinox. These five structures represent the peaks of Mount Meru, the Buddhist, Hindu, and Jain home of divine beings.

Angkor Wat was not always a Buddhist monument. Although the thirteenth-century Chinese traveler Zhou Daguan reported that it was built in a single night by a divine architect, it was actually constructed by King Suryavarman II (1113–c. 1150) to honor the Hindu god Vishnu. The Buddhist king Jayavarman VII's ascent to the throne in 1181 propelled a religious shift, and Angkor Wat evolved into the Buddhist sanctuary it remains today.

By the thirteenth century Buddhist images had replaced much of the Hindu statuary, although hundreds of Hindu bas-reliefs remain. These depict myths, including the "Churning of the Sea of Milk," in which demons and gods use a giant five-headed serpent to extract the elixir of everlasting life from the ocean.

Baekyangsa Temple

Established by Zen Master Yeohwan in 632 CE in the foothills of Mount Baegam-san, Baekyangsa Temple is the center of the Jogye Order, the most representative of Korean Buddhism, combining meditation with sutra studies and practices.

Throughout Asia, where the influence of zodiac animal signs remains strong, the sheep is a symbol of calm and harmony, so it is not a surprise to discover that Baekyangsa means "where even a sheep can perceive the truth." The name refers to a legend that told of a white lamb descending the mountain to listen to a monk chant the Lotus Sutra, and that, upon hearing it, attained Enlightenment and so was able to ascend to heaven. In the Lotus Sutra, the Buddha maps out how all Buddhist paths lead to "the highest summit of Enlightenment," and the lifespan of the Buddha transcends time (giving us the concept of "everywhen;" see page 110).

Build your own temple

This temple is part of South Korea's Templestay experience program, which provides access to temples and monasteries for visits. The idea is to offer a better understanding of Korean culture and Buddhism. These visits include chanting, meditation, the tea ceremony, and pure respite, to help visitors find their "true self." What a privilege it would be to stay at one of them! But not all of us can travel to Korea. How can you build a temple, something the Buddhist teacher Bonnie Myotai Treace calls a place of "hermitage heart," in your life?

Three Sacred Mountains of Dewa

Mount Haguro, Mount Gassan, and Mount Yudono—the Three Sacred Mountains of Dewa—are sacred to many Japanese, and each has a significant shrine.

Making pilgrimages to the mountains was a meaningful ritual for the religions of Shintō and Buddhism, and of particular importance to the Shugendō sect, which evolved in Japan during the seventh century and still practiced today. Shugendō fused the nature-focused religion of Shintōism with Buddhism and later with Taoism. A person who practices Shugendō is called a *yamabushi*, defined as "a person who bows down to the mountains," and as such, their

Experiencing a sacred place

The seventeenth-century haiku master Matsuo Bashō was greatly influenced by the Dewa mountains. In his journals of his travels to the area, translated by Nobuyuki Yuasa, he offers a compelling definition of what it means to be in a sacred place: "As I moved on all fours from rock to rock, bowing reverently at each shrine, I felt the purifying power of this holy environment pervading my whole being." Recall a thin place you have visited. Can you recapture that sensation of its holiness pervading your being?

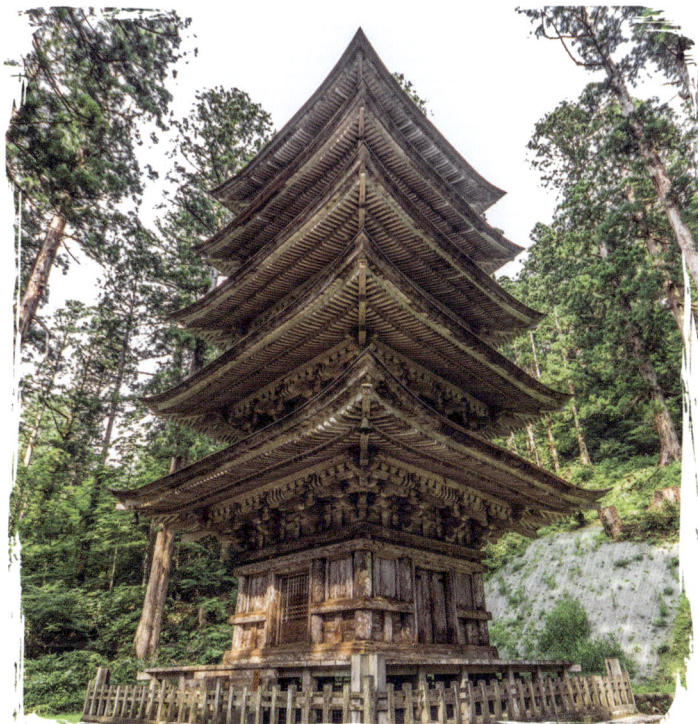

practice focuses on peaks, particularly involving pilgrimages, retreats, and hermitages.

Although Gassan is the tallest of the three mountains, Yudono is seen as the ultimate destination of the *yamabushi's* pilgrimage. This is likely because of the presence of a *goshintai*, an object believed to be connected to a *kami*, or sacred spirit. The *goshintai* on Mount Yudono is a boulder with a hot spring flowing from it.

Waipoua Forest

On the west coast of New Zealand's North Island is the largest remaining tract of native forest in the country, declared a sanctuary in 1952. It is home to giant *kauri* trees, which are treasured by New Zealanders and especially the Indigenous Māori because they are seen as an indicator of the health of the forest and the people who depend on it. Two *kauri* stand out in particular. Tāne Mahuta, named for the Māori god of the forest and of birds, is the largest. It is more than 2,000 years old and still healthy. At over 148 ft (45 m) tall, it deserves its title, "God of the Forest." It grows near Te Matua Ngahere (Father of the Forest), which is the second largest *kauri* tree and is said to have been living even longer—perhaps 3,000 years. Sources say it is the oldest tree in New Zealand and perhaps even on Earth.

Leaf meditation

There's a meditation that I do all the time, especially when I'm in a car or train. I call it "seeing the trees for the forest": *Consider a forest, woods, or a copse. Now pick a single tree. Now focus on one leaf. Think about that leaf—the part it plays in the tree's beauty and nourishment, the way no human may ever touch that leaf, or even look at it.*

This helps me to remember my place in the cosmos. It is a way of putting into practice the words of the Bengali poet and mystic Rabindranath Tagore: "Be still, my heart, these great trees are prayers."

Great Dome of Uluru

Sacred to the Anangu, a group of Aboriginal peoples, this massive sandstone rock formation or "island mountain" in the Australian outback rises 2,820 ft (860 m) above sea level. It is far more than just an impressive rock; within it are small oases, waterholes, and caves, many of which contain petroglyphs and paintings. Important Indigenous sites in Australia and nearby archaeological findings show that humans settled in the area more than 10,000 years ago, about 9,000 years before Europeans arrived.

Uluru is still a sacred place, but for most of us it is best respectfully appreciated from a distance. The Anangu belief system is inextricably linked to Uluru and to the Dreaming or Dreamtime, which is at the very heart of this Indigenous people's heritage and spiritual life. In *The Way of the Earth: Encounters with Nature in Ancient and Contemporary Thought* (1994), the American anthropologist T.C. McLuhan writes: "The Aboriginal landscape consists of a network of traditional pathways—an intricate and sacred criss-crossing of mythical tracks (Dreaming Tracks)—marked by the passages of ancestral

Great Dome of Uluru

beings and punctuated by their legacy of a multitude of holy sites. The Aboriginal people today know these ancestral routes, and when they move across them they are both animating them and honoring their spiritual sources … The maintenance and nurturing of the sites through the vigilant performance of ceremonies and rituals is vital to the health of the tribe and the planet."

Dreamtime is a concept of time that is beginningless and endless. It is all time simultaneously: past, present, and future, or, as the Australian anthropologist W.E.H. Stanner famously described it, "everywhen"—when gods and ancestors traveled over the land and brought it to life, when the universe came into being, creating what became the Aboriginal people's culture. It is believed that Uluru was created by ten ancestors from a featureless place, and that the monolith is the evidence they left of their time on Earth. The paintings and petroglyphs in many of Uluru's caves depict those stories, this Dreaming interconnecting with our times as the Anangu touch the rocks and receive blessings from their still-present ancestors—not worshipped, but revered and relied upon.

The concept of everywhen

Everywhen … I love that word. Think about it: a time before and after simultaneously. Try focusing on a place, any place. It could be your garden, it could be a lake, it could be a geological formation as magnificent and sacred as Uluru. What was there before? And before that? What's there now? Really? And what will come next? Practice experiencing time as nonlinear, not this, then that, but all-at-once, as everywhen, and see what happens.

Taputapuātea Marae

A *marae* is a sacred communal area used for rituals and religious practices as well as social gatherings. *Marae* generally consist of a rectangle of cleared land bordered with stones or wooden posts, and some, including Taputapuātea, include terraces or *paepae* for ceremonial purposes.

Taputapuātea Marae, on the southeastern coast of the island of Raiatea (Bright Sky), is a complex of *marae* that is said to be the birthplace and residence of the gods. It is at the core of the Polynesian people's spiritual life. The original *marae* was established in about the tenth century CE and dedicated to Oro, the god of life and death; it has been a sacred place ever since. Taputapuātea is considered so holy that when *marae* were consecrated on the surrounding islands, stones were taken from it and planted like seeds in the new locations.

Give meaning to found objects

I'm captivated by the idea of planting stones, of bringing a piece of something inanimate to another place to imbue it with its spirit or essence. Perhaps in a way we do this when we bring seashells or remarkable pebbles home from the beach, or when we treasure odd pieces of glass or pottery for no apparent reason. But what if we did this with intent? The next time you're drawn to a rock or a piece of sea glass, pick it up and put it somewhere for another person to find—a windowsill, a subway seat. That way you will act as a secret messenger, transferring the experience of one special place to another.

Goa Gajah or Elephant Cave

Although "Elephant Cave" is the translation of *Goa Gajah*, there are, in fact, no elephants in this temple-cave, which was elaborately carved in the eleventh century, and for that matter there have never been elephants on Bali. Theories abound as to the genesis of the name. Perhaps it is from the stone carving within of Ganesh, the Hindu god with an elephant's head, believed to be the remover of obstacles; or possibly it is from the river nearby, which was once called Lwa Gajah, or "Elephant River." Regardless of the origins of the name, it is believed the cave was built as a place for meditation.

Set in verdant grounds, the temple-cave can be reached only by walking down a long flight of stairs. After passing through a courtyard flanked by seven statues of women holding pitchers of water to represent India's seven holiest rivers—Sarasvati, Yamuna,

Create your own sanctuary

The Elephant Cave was originally created as a sanctuary. The word "sanctuary" comes from the Anglo-French meaning "building set apart for holy worship," and the Latin for "a sacred place, shrine." Consider the concept of sanctuary, a place of spiritual refuge. How can we create space in our lives for healing and contemplation? How responsible are you for creating obstacles to your own sense of sanctuary? Can you remove them? Try setting aside a few minutes each day to grant yourself sanctuary, to be still and experience peace.

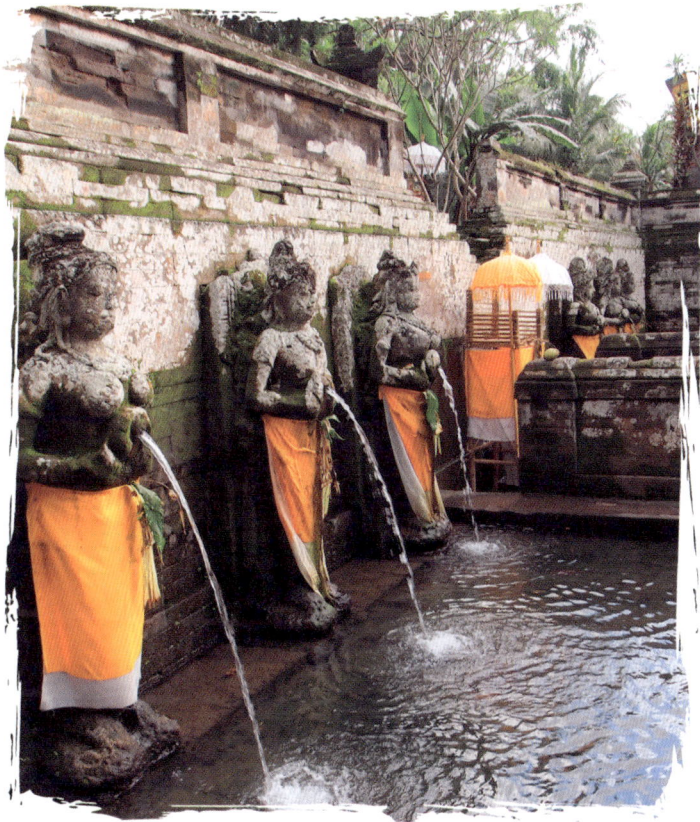

Godavari, Sindhu (Indus), Kaveri, Narmada (Reva), and, of course, the Ganges (see page 86)—visitors are greeted, or perhaps challenged, by stone-carved images of beings, including a giant, making threatening faces to drive away evil spirits.

CHAPTER 4

CARIBBEAN AND CENTRAL & SOUTH AMERICA

GALÁPAGOS ISLANDS
Pacific Ocean

Chichén Itzá

Chichén Itzá is one of the largest Mayan cities ever discovered. It was built in the fifth century CE, flourished, then declined, and was abandoned in 1250. *Chichén* means "at the mouth of the well," and the Itzá were known as water sorcerers or enchanters of the water.

The complex is most famous for its step pyramid, the Temple of Kukulcán—a serpent/bird Mayan deity—which dominates the landscape. Inside the pyramid is an ornate jaguar throne inlaid with jade. During the afternoons of the two equinoxes, the sun casts shadows across the edge of a staircase, and when these shadows reach the statue of a serpent's head, they create the illusion of Kukulcán perched on the exterior wall of the temple.

There are many fascinating structures on the site, including the Group of the Thousand Columns, but there's something else that I find especially intriguing. The entire northern Yucatán Peninsula is a karst—a type of topography formed from soluble rocks such as limestone—with a network of underground rivers. In places where

Hidden beauty

As with the rivers below Chichén Itzá, beautiful things are not always on the surface. Think about beauty that is not revealed at first glance: soil that nurtures new growth, a cocoon about to release a butterfly, rough patches that lead to a more meaningful relationship, the rewards of hard work.

the karst has collapsed, sinkholes or cenotes form, and there are at least four of these in the Chichén Itzá compound. The abundant water (not to mention the remarkable beauty) of these cenotes was likely what drew the Mayans to Chichén.

Island of the Sun

The Isla del Sol (Island of the Sun) is considered one of the most sacred islands in South America. At 5½ sq. miles (14 sq. km), it is the largest of the islands in Lake Titicaca, a freshwater lake between Bolivia and Peru. It is said to be the place to which spirits return at death, and this is because it is considered the birthplace of the Incan bloodline—the origin point for the largest empire in pre-Columbian America. Legends tell that the Incan rulers were sent to Earth by the sun god himself, and that the first Incan, his son, materialized on this island from a crack in the ground. The many ruins dating from the third millennium BCE up to the fifteenth century attest to this; they include the Sacred Rock, a temple likely built by Emperor Topa Inca Yupanqui in the late fifteenth century, as well as a palace and other buildings cut from stone and once surrounded by gardens and fountains.

Sacred origins

Just as spirits are said to begin in and return to Lake Titicaca, every culture, religion, family, and individual has an origin story—a place before which there was no "before." What are your stories? What about the birth of a friendship, a passion, a dream? How can you nurture and celebrate those beginnings?

Machu Picchu

High in the Peruvian Andes, the citadel of Machu Picchu overlooks the Sacred Valley. It was likely constructed as an estate for the Incan emperor Pachacuti in the fifteenth century, as well as a religious, agricultural, and astronomical center, but was abandoned about a century later during the Spanish colonization. Entering via the Sun Gate, the visitor is faced with more than 200 structures, including the Temple of the Sun, the Room of the Three Windows, and the Altar of the Condor, which was used for rituals and as a calendar.

The stones of Machu Picchu were cut with such tremendous precision and assembled so thoughtfully that you cannot even slide a playing card between them. This creates pleasing architecture, but is also practical, because Machu Picchu is in earthquake territory, constructed on two fault lines. During seismic activity the stones "dance," shaking with the landscape but remaining in place.

It is remarkable to consider that all this was accomplished far above sea level in a tropical rainforest reaching into the cloud

Our soul connection

The inseparability from place at Machu Picchu is profound. "No word for 'Nature' (as an abstract concept separate from ourselves) exists in the Quechua language of the Peruvian Andes. Instead, the people say *nuestra naturaleza* (our nature) and [consider it] intimately entwined with their lives," writes T.C. McLuhan. Reflect on this idea. Think about how we are truly part of the *awki* or "soul" of a natural place.

forests. The landscape and all the flora and fauna (hundreds of species of orchid and butterfly, giant hummingbirds, spectacled bears, Andean condors, and, of course, llamas) continue to stir awe, just as they did centuries ago.

Galápagos Islands

The Galápagos is an archipelago of 18 volcanic islands and many rocks and islets west of Ecuador in the Pacific Ocean, straddling the equator. They are famous for their remarkable biodiversity, chronicled by the English naturalist Charles Darwin during the second voyage of HMS *Beagle* in the mid-nineteenth century.

Many of the species on these islands are found nowhere else in the world, heightening the spirituality of the place. These include the giant tortoises, flightless cormorants, marine iguanas, and mockingbirds that Darwin marveled at in his account of the trip from 1845. He was thrilled by the myriad varieties he encountered in this relatively small area, and it famously led to his development of the theory of evolution by natural selection.

Listen to nature

Almost two centuries later, the writer and poet Charlene L. Edge's experience resonated with Darwin's. She describes arriving on one of the islands: "We were standing on a narrow strip of beach, watching sea lions lying around … I could hear the waves on the beach, a low, pulsing swish. Quietly, we just stood there, listening, watching the sleek brown animals, listening, watching for any nearby birds, especially finches. We had to be quiet, and mostly still. This was the basic rule of our life on this trip. 'Just be here now and watch for what might happen.' … Nature was speaking to me, and I wanted to listen." You don't need to travel to the Galápagos to take a moment, pause, and listen to the lessons of nature.

Easter Island

One of the geologically youngest and most remote places on Earth, this volcanic island was given its name by the Dutch explorer Jacob Roggeveen on Easter Day in 1722. It had been settled centuries before, likely around 400 CE, by Polynesians known as the Rapa Nui, whose civilization included agriculture and animal husbandry. It is as sculptors of the sacred that they are best known; almost 900 monuments called *moai*, made from porous volcanic rock, ranging in size from 6 to 60 ft (about 2–20 m or three stories) high, were carved with axes, perhaps to honor ancestors, stand guard around the quarry in which they were created, or mark burial sites.

For centuries, these colossi were thought to be giant heads and people speculated about why they were created and how. Why just heads? It seemed a mystery—until, in the late twentieth century, American archaeologists discovered that buried below the surface were full torsos that had been hidden over time.

The things that are unseen are eternal

The Apostle Paul wrote to the Corinthians, "We look not to the things that are seen but to the things that are unseen. For the things that are seen are transient, but the things that are unseen are eternal." Perhaps that's the lesson of Easter Island: not to make fleeting assumptions, but to be present until the mystery is revealed.

Monquirá Archaeological Park

Monquirá Archaeological Park is the most important remaining site of the pre-Columbian Muisca or Chibcha culture. At the time of the Spanish invasion in the mid-sixteenth century, these Indigenous peoples were well established, with a population of as many as three million and an economy that included agriculture, gold and salt mining, and trading. Yet the Spanish named the area El Infiernito, meaning "Little Hell." Although dismissed as a pagan site by the conquistadors, this was for the original inhabitants a sacred place and pilgrimage destination as long ago as 2000 BCE.

This is an active archaeological site, and discoveries are continually being made there. This vast expanse in the high plateaus of the Colombian Andes includes dozens of standing stones and monoliths, several burial mounds, and a subterranean altar that was used for religious ceremonies. Many of the stones were aligned with

Under the same sky

I love imagining how the Muisca, the Druids or Romans at Stonehenge (see page 10), and the Northern Plains Indians (see page 136) all calculated, studied, and gazed at the same planets and stars, the very ones we now see years later. To me it is a clear testimony to human interconnection and planetary interdependence. As different as our lives may be, we all still gaze at the same sky.

the sun and the moon, creating an observatory to calculate natural phenomena such as equinoxes that heralded the rainy season. At certain points during the Earth's orbit round the sun, the shadows of the columns align with Lake Iguaque, said to be the birthplace of the Muiscan mother goddess. Their astronomical calculations were advanced, and aided with planting and harvesting.

Atacama Desert

The Atacama Desert is said to be the driest non-polar desert on the planet. Not only is it a desert as we generally understand the term— arid terrain without much vegetation—but more specifically it is a fog desert, where droplets from condensation (instead of rain) provide most of the moisture necessary to sustain life. This 41,000-sq.-mile (106,000-sq.-km) strip of land reaching from the Pacific Coast west to the Andes, punctuated by Licancabur, a volcano considered a holy mountain by the Atacameño people, is also said to be the best place in the world for stargazing. Its high altitude and the absence of both air and light pollution and cloud cover make it an astronomer's paradise.

However, a telescope is not a requirement for stargazing in the Atacama. Centuries before the Europeans arrived in South America, the Indigenous peoples of the region charted the sun, constellations, and planets in order to navigate time and terrain. They relied on the Southern Cross, the southern hemisphere's most famous constellation, as well as the Llama, one of the most important constellations for the Inca, which rises in November with the stars Alpha and Beta Centauri serving as its "eyes."

Who are you?

The great twentieth-century Chilean poet Pablo Neruda wrote, "Who writes your name with letters of smoke among the southern stars? Oh, let me memorize you how you were then, when you did not yet exist." His words evoke the well-known Zen koan: "What was your original face before your parents were born?" Think about this. Who are you beyond the stars; who were you before you were conceived?

Church of la Compañía de Jesús

The Church of la Compañía de Jesús is one of the most significant works of Spanish Baroque architecture in South America. The carvings of its main façade were executed entirely in Ecuadorian volcanic stone called andesite, but it is renowned throughout the world for the mineral decorating its vast interior: gold. Seven tons of it—gold leaf and gilded carvings in plaster and wood—earned the church the nickname "Quito's Sistine Chapel."

Construction began soon after the Jesuit priests arrived in the city presently known as Quito in 1586, but it was a slow process, taking more than 160 years. The builders incorporated architectural elements from several cultures. Ornate Baroque and Churrigueresque (Spanish Baroque) are most prominent, along with Moorish influence in the geometric forms decorating the pillars, and Neoclassical style in the Chapel of St Mariana de Jesús.

This syncretism (the amalgamation of religions, mythologies, and cultures) is not solely European. Throughout the building are representations of the Indigenous peoples and nature who predated the colonists by millennia. The sun symbol on the entrance door and ceiling perhaps invites the Incan population to enter the church, and there are Ecuadorian plants and faces in the carvings on walls and pillars. Its beauty combined with the mixture of cultures gives the church a uniquely spiritual and eclectic feeling.

The source of your beliefs

In *Psychotherapy East and West* (1961), the English writer and theologian Alan W. Watts wrote: "Those who rove freely through the various traditions, accepting what they can use and rejecting what they cannot, are condemned as undisciplined syncretists. But the use of one's reason is not a lack of discipline, nor is there any important religion which is not itself a syncretism, a 'growing up together' of ideas and practices of diverse origin." I think about this all the time. Just as you might wonder where your fruit, vegetables, or wine was sourced, think about where your beliefs come from.

CHAPTER 5

NORTH AMERICA

LAKE LOUISE
Banff National Park, Alberta, Canada

Moose Mountain Medicine Wheel

Moose Mountain, in the southeastern corner of the state of Saskatchewan, is actually mostly a plateau. It has been peopled for about 11,000 years as a sacred site for Northern Plains Indians, likely since the Blackfeet Nation, the first of the current Indian groups on the plains of what are now called Saskatchewan and Alberta, arrived in about 800 CE.

For more than 2,000 years, the medicine wheel or sacred hoop on Moose Mountain has been a place of healing and practice. As with the standing stones of the United Kingdom, there are many theories about why medicine wheels were constructed. Were they built to chart astronomical and solar alignments, or to predict the return of migrating herds such as buffalo, or perhaps for their symbolism as a place for offering, burial, or gathering ingredients for medicines? About 150 medicine wheels still exist throughout Indigenous lands in North America. Moose Mountain is one of the largest—its outer circumference is 30 ft (9 m) in diameter, its spokes reaching as far as 123 ft (37 m)—making it about twice the size of the famous medicine wheel in Bighorn, Wyoming.

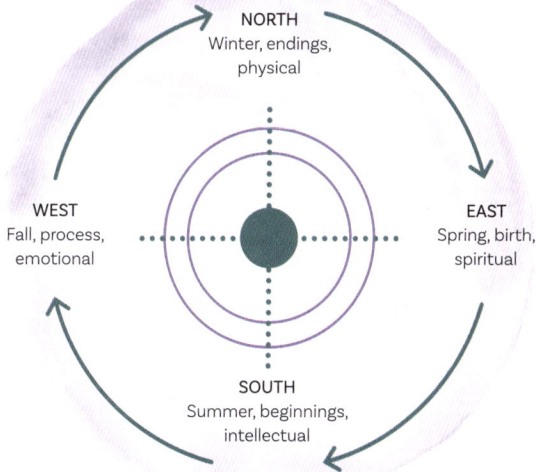

NORTH
Winter, endings,
physical

EAST
Spring, birth,
spiritual

WEST
Fall, process,
emotional

SOUTH
Summer, beginnings,
intellectual

Seek spiritual balance

For Indigenous Americans, medicine is that which heals the spiritual self. These wheels or hoops represent the spiritual connection between earth and sky. Each tribe interprets the structure of the medicine wheel in a distinct way, but a generalized key to the four cardinal points is shown in the chart above.

Consider engaging with these parts of a cycle in your life. It could be through four columns in a journal, or through paying attention to the direction of the wheel during meditation. What shifts when you do? Is the spiritual balanced with the intellectual? Are you as thoughtful about closings and endings as you are about beginnings?

Black Hills

This isolated mountain range, named directly from the Lakota *ha sapa* (black hills), includes Black Elk Peak (7,244 ft/2,208 m), the highest point east of the Rocky Mountains. Black Hills National Forest is on the western edge of the state of South Dakota, spanning more than 1,950 sq. miles (5,050 sq. km), blanketed

Sacred geography

Thinking about sacred geography and the lessons of the Native North Americans is a meaningful practice. No matter where you are, someone was in that physical space before you. Consider this as you move about your day, your world, your life.

in ponderosa pine and dotted with herds of bison and remarkable geological structures.

Formerly Harney Peak, Black Elk Peak was given a new name in 2016. William S. Harney was a general in the Mexican–American and Indian wars, and this etymology was abandoned in favor of honoring the original inhabitants of the region. The new name recognizes the legendary Lakota Sioux medicine man, as well as the state's important Native American communities.

T.C. McLuhan wrote in *The Way of the Earth*: "Sacred geography is a fundamental ingredient of Native North American religious beliefs and practices. The idea of the sacred is founded upon a profound knowledge, understanding, and conviction of the inherent sanctity of all things. Entering sacredness is the universal goal of all American Indian ritual." This is far more than a theory, and nowhere is it more evident than in the Black Hills, which remain a hub and heart for rituals, including the Sun Dance (a community ceremony and prayer for healing) and vision questions (a rite of passage usually carried out by young men entering adulthood), particularly among the Lakota peoples.

Lake Louise

Lake Louise, a vast, serene glacial lake in the Canadian Rockies, is called Ho-run-num-nay (Lake of the Little Fishes) by the Stoney Nakoda First Nations people, who have inhabited the area for more than 10,000 years, fishing, hunting bison and other animals, gathering sacred herbs, and finding spiritual and physical healing in the hot springs.

Lake Louise is famed for its remarkably turquoise waters. This almost unearthly blue is the result of something called rock flour or glacial flour, which occurs when lakes are fed by glacier melt instead of rivers. In addition to transporting large stones and boulders, glaciers pulverize stones and minerals in their path, forming a fine-grained silt and clay. The finest particles resemble flour

Places of energy

Many people hypothesize that Lake Louise is an energy vortex, a power point on a series of energetic grids or ley lines. In Jini Reddy's book *Wanderland* (2020), Elen Sentier, a self-described British Native shaman, defines a ley line as "an ancient thoroughfare, part of a network that takes in … standing stones, church sites, and prominent natural features." Perhaps Lake Louise, Stonehenge, the Ganges, and Uluru (see pages 10, 86, and 108) are all connected. Is there a pattern to the world's energy points? What about in your life? Are there places you're drawn to for reasons you can't explain?

in appearance and remain suspended in the water. When sunlight strikes the water, these particles absorb the shortest wavelengths—purples and indigos—and scatter the longer ones—reds and yellows—meaning we see the blues and greens more clearly.

Mauna Kea

According to Indigenous Hawaiian beliefs, the island of Hawaii is itself a holy place. Mauna Kea, an ancient volcano that has been dormant for about five million years, is no exception. Located at the northern end of the island, it is 13,803 ft (4,207 m) above sea level, but if measured from the Pacific Ocean floor it is the tallest mountain on the planet, rising 33,474 ft (10,203 m). Ancient Hawaiians hunted and foraged in the forests of *māmane* and *naio*

(tree species that are endemic to the island) on the higher slopes and *koa* on the lower.

Mauna Kea is honored as an ancestor, so it is not just a landscape feature but part of native Hawaiian genealogy, making it perhaps the most sacred element of the culture. It is seen as the temple abode and physical manifestation of Kane, the creator deity, as well as other divine beings and ancestors. In mythology it is the place where the Sky Father and Earth Mother meet. This understanding of place is not mere myth but an active understanding.

A ritual of forgiveness

When I first learned of the Hawaiian practice of Ho'oponopono, I was instantly drawn to the concept. The Hawaiian Dictionary defines it as "To put to rights; to put in order or shape, correct, revise, adjust, amend, regulate, arrange, rectify, tidy up, make orderly or neat ... to make ready, as canoemen preparing to catch a wave." It continues by explaining that it is a "mental cleansing ... through prayer, discussion, confession, repentance, and mutual restitution and forgiveness." As I understand it, the crux of Ho'oponopono is forgiveness. The process is generally engaged in as a community or group, and has several steps:

Begin with a prayer to set intention.

Make a statement of the problem. What needs forgiveness? Who was hurt? What were the consequences of the actions?

Discuss this problem in a spirit of cooperation, not fault. Acknowledge each participant's feelings and reactions, allowing for remorse and confession.

Pause to reflect on the conversation.

As a group, release this past act together, perhaps incorporating a ritual symbolic of this passage through forgiveness to unity.

Although this is traditionally a group practice, try adapting it as a personal ritual or meditation as a path to forgiving others or yourself.

Mount Shasta

Mount Shasta is a volcano, and although it hasn't erupted for hundreds of years, it is still technically active. At 10,000 ft (3,000 m) high, it is the second largest volcano in the Cascade Mountains. On a clear day, it is visible from the floor of Central Valley some 100 miles (161 km) away.

In 1874, in *Letters to a Friend*, the Scots-American naturalist John Muir described Mount Shasta in winter beautifully: "When I first caught sight of it over the braided folds of the Sacramento Valley, I was fifty miles [80 km] away and afoot, alone, and weary, yet all my blood turned to wine and I have not been weary since." Travelers and locals before and since seem to concur that there's a magic to Mount Shasta.

At the time of Euro-American contact in the 1820s, the Native American tribes who lived within view of this impressive mountain included the Shasta, Okwanuchu, Modoc, Achomawi, Atsugewi, Karuk, Klamath, Wintu, and Yana tribes. Their ancestors had been

Healing and awe

I've met many people who have been to Mount Shasta, and regardless of heritage or the purpose of their journey, all have returned healed and awestruck. Perhaps awe is a synthesis of the natural and the imagined, of science and mystery. A bird at a feeder, an especially choppy ocean, or a newborn child can all inspire awe.

there for more than 7,000 years, and were well established in the area. Many of them believed that the Spirit of the Above-World dwelled on Mount Shasta before he descended to do battle with the Spirit of the Below-World. The area has continued to draw the spiritually inclined, and now features places of present-day Native American ritual as well as monasteries both Catholic and Buddhist, and places of worship for churches from the Unitarian to the Church of Jesus Christ of Latter-Day Saints. It is no wonder that more than one Native American elder has described the land as "a living church" as sacred as Mecca, Machu Picchu (see page 122), Bodh Gaya (see page 81), or Jerusalem.

Congo Square

Congo Square has been known by many names, among them Place Publique, Beauregard Square, Circus Place, Congo Park, and Place d'Armes. It is an open space in what is now Louis Armstrong Park in Tremé, New Orleans, a neighborhood with a rich history of African-American music. During Louisiana's colonial era, Congo Square served as a gathering place for free and enslaved Africans on Sunday afternoons, and at one time it was the sole place offering at least a modicum of religious freedom and cultural expression, for dancing, drumming circles, and ceremonies. A spirit of communion exists there to this day, as Caribbean and European cultures have mingled, evolving into the jazz of Louis Armstrong and Wynton Marsalis, Nellie Lutcher and Louis Prima, as well as the music of Mardi Gras traditions and Second Line community parades awash with handkerchiefs and parasols.

The collective power of music

Music unites spirit with time and place, individuals and communities, all through the breath of aural poetry. Hold that thought the next time you hear a song on the radio or sing where you worship, and consider the interconnection that music embodies. Go beyond the words to all the people the music has touched, and how an arrangement of sounds and rhythm and words has inextricably woven through the course of their lives ... and yours.

As the jazz musician and composer Sidney Bechet wrote in his autobiography, *Treat It Gentle* (1960): "All those people who had been slaves … it was like they were trying to find out in this music what they were supposed to do with this freedom: playing the music and listening to it—waiting for it to express what they needed to learn, once they had learned it wasn't just white people the music had to reach to, nor even to their own people, but straight out to life, to what a man does with his life when it finally *is* his." It is this music of freedom within the context of self—and one could say *Self* or perhaps soul—that echoes in Congo Square today.

Old Quaker Meeting House

As you make your way up chaotic Northern Boulevard in the heart of Flushing, a neighborhood where the traffic is relentless and every bit of space is crammed with businesses and people, concrete and racket, the words "spiritual" and "sacred" are likely not the first to come to mind. Yet, as you near the Quaker Meeting House you will notice a few oaks and elms tucked between the buildings, and entering through a gate and abandoning the bustle transports you to quite a different place and time.

Unlike the land it sits on, the Quaker Meeting House has not changed much since it was built in the late seventeenth and early eighteenth centuries. It is the oldest place of worship still standing in New York State, a rough-hewn, wood-frame structure that silently encompasses the history of both the place and the Religious Society of Friends, known less formally as the Quakers. The sect was founded in England in the seventeenth century by George Fox, who preached "seeking the inner light" in all people through integrity, equality, simplicity, community, stewardship of the Earth, and a commitment to peace. Evidence of this call can be found next to the meeting house where a burial ground containing hundreds of graves includes those of several American abolitionists, among them William Burling and Matthew Franklin.

Be an example to others

In a letter to ministers, George Fox wrote: "Be patterns, be examples in all countries, places, islands, nations, wherever you come, that your carriage and life may preach among all sorts of people, and to them; then you will come to walk cheerfully over the world." Be inspired by this universal sense of the sacred that spans the planet's countries, places, islands, and nations.

Selected Bibliography and References

Adams, Mark. "Machu Picchu Secrets." *National Geographic*, May 2021.

Adomaitis, Nerijus. "Lithuania Cross-Makers Keep Tradition Alive." *Reuters*, May 28, 2008.

Angier, Natalie. "Michelangelo, Renaissance Man of the Brain, Too?" *NY Times*, October 10, 1990.

Anyumba, Godfrey, & M. Nkuna. "Lake Fundudzi…" *African Hospitality, Tourism & Leisure*. 2017.

Barthold, Vasilii V. *Historical Geography of Iran*. Princeton University Press, 2016.

Bashō, Matsuo. *The Narrow Road to the Deep North…* Penguin, 2010.

Batchelor, Stephen. "Meaning of the Buddha's Birth." stephenbatchelor.org.

Baxter, Sarah. *Spiritual Places*. Aurum Press, 2018.

BBC Studios. "Magic Mushrooms & Reindeer." YouTube, January 26, 2009.

Begg, Ean. *Cult of the Black Virgin*. Chiron Publishing, 2013.

Bosworth, C. E., et al. *Encyclopaedia of Islam*. Brill, 1997.

Bower, Bruce. "Stonehenge Enhanced Sounds…" *Science News*. September, 2020.

Buonarroti, Michaelangelo, & T. Campanella. *Sonnets*. Smith, Elder, 1878.

Butterfield, Fox. "China's Majestic Huang Shan." *NY Times*, February 8, 1981.

Chami, Maximilian F., & F.A. "Management of Sacred Heritage Places in Tanzania." *Heritage Management*. 2020.

Chatwin, Bruce. *The Songlines*. Open Road Media, 2016.

Clark, Trish. *Good Night God Bless*. HiddenSpring, 2008.

"Colors of the Arab World." Arab America, December, 2019.

Corbin, Amy. "Mauna Kea." Sacred Land Film Project, August, 2014.

Covarrubias, Miguel. *Island of Bali*. Tuttle, 2015.

Dauphin, Lauren. "How Glaciers Turn Lakes Turquoise." Earth Observatory. May, 2019.

David. "Incidental Naturalist." June 5, 2019. incidentalnaturalist.com.

David, Trevor. "Medicine Wheels of North America." *Atlas Obscura*, February, 2013.

de Boer, J.Z. "Delphi Was a Gas!" Geology, August, 2001.

"Derek Blyth's Hidden Secrets of Brussels." *Brussels Times*, July 4, 2020.

Devy, G.N., et al. *The Language Loss of the Indigenous*. Routledge, 2016.

Di Bella, Stefano, et al. "'Delivery' of Adam." *Mayo Clinic Proceedings* 90, 2015.

Dillon, Cathy. "Hiking to the Tiger's Nest, Bhutan." Earth Trekkers, August, 2021.

Dongyal Rinpoche Khenpo Tsewang. "Eight Emanations of Guru Padmasambhava." Turtle Hill, 1992.

Drummond, William H. *Giants' Causeway*. Longman, Hurst, et al, 1811.

Dubois, Thomas A. *Introduction to Shamanism*. Cambridge University Press, 2009.

Dulewich, Jenna. "Stoney Ceremony Commemorates Untold Lake Louise History." *Rocky Mountain Outlook*, August, 2020.

Duricy, Michael. "Black Madonnas." All About Mary. University of Dayton.

Eck, Diana L. *Banaras, City of Light.* Columbia University Press, 1999.

"Fauna & Flora." Foundation Sonian Forest, 2020. sonianforest.be.

Fenech, Louis E., & W.H. McLeod. *Historical Dictionary of Sikhism.* Rowman & Littlefield, 2014.

Fleischman, Paul R. *Wonder: When & Why the World Appears Radiant.* Small Batch Books, 2013.

Fonneland, Trude A., et al. *Sámi Religion: Identities, Practices & Dynamics.* MDPI, 2020.

Franco, Ángela. "Synagogue of Santa Maria la Blanca." Museum with No Frontiers, 2021.

"Glacial till & Glacial Flour." National Parks Service, February, 2018.

Grandtner, Miroslav M., & J. Chevrette. *Dictionary of Trees...* Elsevier, 2014.

Gross, Daniel A. "This Is Your Brain on Silence." *Nautilus.* August, 2014.

Higgins, Charlotte. "Battle for the Future of Stonehenge." *Guardian*, February 8, 2019.

Hind, Rebecca. *Sacred Places: Sites of Spirituality & Faith.* Carlton, 2012.

"Hortense Leandita Hamilton (1853–1874)." Find a Grave, November, 2015.

"Huangshan: Mountain of 20,000 Poems." ANU College of Asia & the Pacific. April, 2017.

Huffman, Thomas N. "Mapungubwe & Great Zimbabwe." *Anthropological Archaeology* 28. 2009.

"Il-Maqluba, Qrendi, Malta." geulogy.com

"Is This the Belgian Stonehenge?" *Discovering Belgium*, August, 2020.

Jeffers, Robinson. Letter. *The Wild God of the World* (2003), edited by Albert Gelpi.

Jenkins, Mark. Book of Marvels: *An Explorer's Miscellany.* National Geographic Society, 2009.

Juahari, Parul. "Sal Tree: From Enlightenment to Economy." Rachnakar, July, 2021.

Jung, C.G., et al. *Collected Works of C.G. Jung*, Volume 9. Princeton University Press, 2014.

Jung, C.G., & J.L. Jarrett. *Nietzsche's Zarathustra.* Routledge, 1989.

Kazantzakis, Nikos, & P.A. Bien. *Report to Greco.* Faber, 2001.

Kennedy, Maev. "Glastonbury Thorn Chopped..." *Guardian*, December 9, 2010.

Khyentse, Jamyang. *Best Foot Forward: A Pilgrim's Guide to the Sacred Sites of the Buddha.* Shambhala, 2018.

Kraft, Siv Ellen. "Spiritual Activism. Saving Mother Earth in Sápmi." *Religions* 11. 2020.

"Lake Fundudzi & Mashovhela Rock Pool." Morning Sun, November, 2018.

Langley, Jill. "Discover the Mysterious Lake Fundudzi." Stray Along the Way, July, 2021.

"Larnaca Salt Lake." Ramsar Sites Information Service, January, 2008.

Leary, Catie. "Sacred Mountain Peaks." Treehugger, June, 2021.

Li, Rebecca. *Allow Joy into Our Hearts: Chan Practice in Uncertain Times.* Winterhead, 2021.

"Mahamuni Temple, Mandalay, Myanmar." orientalarchitecture.com.

Mahdi Nejad, J., et al. "Study on the Concepts & Themes of Color & Light in the Exquisite Islamic Architecture." *Fundamental & Applied Sciences* 8. 2018.

Martin, Martin, D. Monro. *Description of the Western Islands of Scotland,* Ca. 1695... Edinburgh: Birlinn, 2010.

Martin-Brown, Joan, et al. *Historic Cities & Sacred Sites.* World Bank, 2001.

McLuhan, Teri C. *Cathedrals of the Spirit: The Message of Sacred Places.* Thorsons, 1996.

McLuhan, Teri. C. *The Way of the Earth: Encounters with Nature in Ancient & Contemporary Thought.* Simon & Schuster, 1994.

Meng, Yang. "Yungang Grottoes Opens One More Cave with Statue of Buddha & His Son." *CGTN.* August, 2021.

Meshberger, Frank Lynn. "Interpretation of Michelangelo's Creation of Adam Based on Neuroanatomy." *JAMA:* 264. 1990

Modak, Sebastian. "On a Remote Siberian Island Asking, Was It Just a Dream?" *NY Times,* November 5, 2019.

Muir, John. *Letters to a Friend.* Houghton Mifflin, 1915.

Ngarantja, Tjukurpa K. "Uluru-Kata Tjuta National Park." 2020.

Nicholls, Christine Judith. "'Dreamtime' & 'the Dreaming.'" *The Conversation,* September, 2021.

Nicholls, Ethan. "King Arthur's Tomb." *Atlas Obscura,* September, 2018.

Nikitin, Pavel. "Rainbow of Baikal Travel." May, 2014.

Onishi, Norimitsu. "Ethiopia's Rock of Ages, Balm of the Faithful." *NY Times,* August 2, 2001.

"Our Story." Shasta Indian Nation. shastaindiannation.org.

Parlow, Anita. *Cry, Sacred Ground: Big Mountain.* Christic Institute, 1988.

Porter, Lewis, et al. Jazz: *From Its Origins to the Present.* Prentice Hall, 1993.

Pukui, Mary Kawena, et al. *Hawaiian Dictionary.* University of Hawaii Press, 1991.

Rao, Desiraju Hanumanta. "Bala Kanda—Youthful Majesties." Valmiki Ramayana, September 2002.

Rasmussen, Susan J. "Tuareg." *Encyclopedia of World Culture.* G.K. Hall. 1996.

Robinson, Francis. *Atlas of the Islamic World.* Facts On File, 1982.

"Rock-Hewn Churches, Lalibela." African World Heritage Sites, 2018.

Rodin, Auguste, & P. Gsell. *Art: Conversations with Paul Gsell.* University of California Press, 1984.

"R.S. Thomas." Poets' Graves. poetsgraves.co.uk/thomas_rs.htm.

Rūmī, Jalāl Al-Dīn, & R. Abdulla. *Words of Paradise.* Viking, 2000.

"Sami in Sweden." Swedish Institute, June, 2021.

Scherrer, Deborah. "Medicine Wheels & Cultural Connections." Stanford Solar Center. 2015.

Schilling, Govert. "Astronomer's Paradise, Chile..." Smithsonian Magazine, July, 2015.

"Scotland's New Age Outpost..." *NZ Herald*, June 13, 2001.

"Seven Line Prayer of Guru Rinpoche." www.shambhala.com.

Sharma, Arvind. *Goddesses & Women in the Indic Religious Tradition*. Brill, 2005.

Shelemay, Kay K. "Zēmā: A Concept of Sacred Music in Ethiopia." *World of Music* 24. 1982.

Shipton, Ceri, et al. "Reinvestigation of Kuumbi Cave, Zanzibar..." *Azania: Archaeological Research in Africa* 51. 2016.

Smith, Huston. *Illustrated World's Religions*. HarperOne, 1995.

Smithies, Richard. "Temples of Angkor Wat & the Search for Meaning in Life." *Works & Conversations*, May, 2020.

Thomas, R.S., & J. Cotter. *Etched by Silence*. Canterbury Press, 2013.

Thoreau, Henry David, & D. Searls. *Journals of Henry David Thoreau*, 1837–1861.

Tregaskis, Moana. "Temples Hewn from Rock in India." *NY Times*, October 23, 1988.

Tyson, Neil deGrasse. *Death By Black Hole*. W.W. Norton & Company, 2014.

van Adel, Tinde. "How African-based Winti Belief Helps to Protect Forests..." *Sacred Natural Sites*. Earthscan.

van der Geer, Alexandra, et al. *Evolution of Island Mammals*. Wiley Blackwell, 2021.

Walsh, William Thomas. Our Lady of Fátima. Doubleday, 1990.

Watts, Alan. *Psychotherapy, East & West*. Vintage, 1975.

Weiner, Eric. *Man Seeks God*. Twelve, 2011.

Westwood, Jennifer. *Atlas of Mysterious Places*. Grove, 1987.

Wharton, Edith. *In Morocco*. Macmillan, 1920.

Williamson, Hugh Ross, & Clare Leighton. *The Flowering Hawthorn*. Neumann Press, 1999.

Yanko, Dave. "Endangered Stones." Virtual Saskatchewan Online Magazine.

Žemaitis, Augustinas. "Hill of Crosses." True Lithuania. 2020.

Index

Photography Credits

© Shutterstock.com and the listed contributors:

pp. 1, 85: Luciano Mortula - LGM

pp. 2 center, 87: CherylRamalho

pp. 2 bottom, 127: Erlantz P.R

pp. 3, 33: kav38

pp. 3, 146: Mark Baldwin

pp. 8, 15: Nuaehnaja

p. 11: David Herraez Calzada

p. 13: irisphoto1

p. 17: orxy

p. 20-21: MNStudio

p. 23: Sophie Leguil

p. 25: Roman Evgenev

p. 27: Tomas Indrak

p. 29: Ana Flasker

p. 30: Miks Mihails Ignats

p. 37: pabloavanzini

p. 38: Stas Moroz

p. 41: RPBaiao

p. 43: JJFarq

p. 45: Zvonimir Atletic

p. 47: Alberto Loyo

pp. 50-51: Jamo Images

p. 52: Kiev.Victor

p. 53: Bernhard Richter

p. 55: muratart

p. 59: Waj

p. 61: Dmitry Pichugin

p. 63: DanielW

p. 64: Boris Stroujko

p. 67: WitR

p. 70: doleesi

pp. 76-77, 89: Giusparta

p. 79: Mazur Travel

p. 82: Alexandra Lande

p. 90: flocu

p. 93: Saknarong Tayaset

p. 94: HM Shahidul Islam

p. 99: Ralf Siemieniec

p. 100: Sergey Peterman

p. 103: The Mariner 4291

p. 105: Manuel Ascanio

pp. 107, 109: Stanislav Fosenbauer

p. 113: maloff

p. 115: Takashi Images

pp. 116-117, 124: Seumas Christie-Johnston

p. 119: Danilo Ascione

p. 121: NiarKrad

p. 123: San Hoyano

p. 129: OSTILL is Franck Camhi

p. 131: Fotografo de los Andes

p. 132: Santiago Salinas

p. 137 (circle illustration): Tamara Kulikova

p. 138: Iryna Marienko

p. 141: Club4traveler

pp. 142-143: Juergen_ Wallstabe

p. 149: William A. Morgan Box frames: phipatbig and alanadesign

Other contributors

p. 75 © Rod Waddington

p. 151 © John Choe, Flushing Monthly Meeting of the Religious Society of Friends, flushingfriends.org

Acknowledgments

It was such a delight to work again with the wise and patient team at CICO Books, especially Kristine Pidkameny, Carmel Edmonds, and Cindy Richards. I am so grateful you sent me on this adventure and helped me navigate the way. Many thanks as well to Duane Stapp who is always my best first reader, to Tyl Stapp who helped me picture the journeys, and to Larry Shapiro for his many thoughtful reading recommendations. Gratitude as well to Crystal Sershen, Charlene Edge, Emily Francis, Miles Neale, Teresa Cavanaugh, Christina Harcar, Deborah Wolk, Chris Grosso, Rebecca Li, Magdalen Beiting, and Elsie and William Peck. Gratitude to T.C. McLuhan, whose writing provided much inspiration. This book is dedicated to Ruth Mullen whose brilliance, joy, and friendship I miss every day.